BIM for Landscape

Building Information Modelling (BIM) is transforming working practices across the built environment sector, as clients, professionals, contractors and manufacturers throughout the supply chain grasp the opportunities that BIM presents. The first book ever to focus on the implementation of BIM processes in landscape and external works, *BIM for Landscape* will help landscape professionals understand what BIM means for them. This book is intended to equip landscape practitioners and practices to meet the challenges and reap the rewards of working in a BIM environment – and to help professionals in related fields to understand how BIM processes can be brought into landscape projects. BIM offers significant benefits to the landscape profession, and heralds a new chapter in interdisciplinary relationships. *BIM for Landscape* shows how BIM can enhance collaboration with other professionals and clients, streamline information processes, improve decision-making and deliver well-designed landscape projects that are right first time, on schedule and on budget.

This book looks at the organisational, technological and professional practice implications of BIM adoption. It discusses in detail the standards, structures and information processes that form BIM Level 2-compliant workflows, highlighting the role of the landscape professional within the new ways of working that BIM entails. It also looks in depth at the digital tools used in BIM projects, emphasising the 'information' in Building Information Modelling, and the possibilities that data-rich models offer in landscape design, maintenance and management. *BIM for Landscape* will be an essential companion to the landscape professional at any stage of their BIM journey.

The Landscape Institute is the professional body for landscape architects. It is an educational charity and chartered body responsible for protecting, conserving and enhancing the natural and built environment for the benefit of the public. It champions well-designed and well-managed urban and rural landscape to inspire great places where people want to live, work and visit. To find out more about the Landscape Institute, visit www.landscapeinstitute.org

BIM for Landscape

The Landscape Institute

Routledge
Taylor & Francis Group

LONDON AND NEW YORK

Landscape Institute

Inspiring great places

First published 2016
by Routledge
2 Park Square, Milton Park, Abingdon, Oxon OX14 4RN

and by Routledge
711 Third Avenue, New York, NY 10017

Routledge is an imprint of the Taylor & Francis Group, an informa business

© 2016 The Landscape Institute

British Library Cataloguing-in-Publication Data
A catalogue record for this book is available from the British Library

Library of Congress Cataloging-in-Publication Data
A catalog record for this book has been requested

ISBN: 978-1-138-79668-3 (hbk)
ISBN: 978-1-315-75771-1 (ebk)

Typeset in Frutiger
by Keystroke, Station Road, Codsall, Wolverhampton
Printed by Bell & Bain Ltd, Glasgow

Contents

Figures

Preface

I welcome this book. It is timely and demonstrates the landscape profession's leadership in the field. It will be a helpful resource, not only for landscape practitioners, but also for fellow professionals in related fields starting to understand the application of BIM to landscape works. This will provide an invaluable early guide to elements of good practice.

Noel Farrer, PLI
President of the Landscape Institute

Foreword

Our built environment is becoming increasingly digitised, with an ever-greater use of computer-readable data to help achieve better outcomes throughout all stages of the project life cycle. BIM is helping facilitate this shift towards a digitised sector, bringing a strong emphasis on the use of shareable asset information to support the better creation and care of our assets, including our public realm, and inspiring places where people want to live, work and visit.

BIM is helping us move towards a construction industry that builds right the first time, has good productivity, and the ability to create landscapes, buildings and infrastructure that give people and society the added value we need. In the UK, the Government Construction Strategy and its requirement for BIM Level 2 on all centrally procured projects has undoubtedly helped accelerate this journey, and facilitate the creation of a suite of world-leading standards for the management and exchange of digital data.

BIM lets us generate design options rapidly, visualise better, and simulate and test early in the pre-construction stages. This is not a simple case of re-tooling, but thinking more about defining and managing our data to support the decision-making process in the context of a Common Data Environment. Central to this is a collaborative way of working, with a clear unified purpose and defined information exchanges.

It is important, as we make this shift, that clear and simple guidance is available to the various communities of practice that make up our industry, to help demystify and to give practical advice on starting the journey, or to help accelerate it towards a digitised and virtualised landscape process. This book will undoubtedly help practices and individuals no matter where they are in their BIM journey.

David Philp MSc BSc FICE FRICS FCIOB FCInstES FGBC
BIM Director AECOM EMEA&I and Chair Scottish BIM Delivery Group

Acknowledgements

Authored by Henry Fenby-Taylor for the Landscape Institute.
Advised by the LI BIM Working Group, chaired by Simon Bell and Mike Shilton.

The Landscape Institute and the BIM Working Group are grateful to all the companies, organisations and individuals who contributed their time, knowledge and expertise to this book. Particular thanks are due to Arup, Arup Associates, Birmingham City University, CS Design Software, Colour UDL, HLM, HOK, Keysoft Solutions Ltd., LDA Design, Marshalls plc, the NBS and Vectorworks Inc.

Image credits

Copyright material reproduced with kind permission from:

BIM Task Group I 8.1, 8.3, 8.4
British Standards Institution I 11.2, 11.3, 11.4, 18.1, 18.2
Colour Urban Design Ltd I 1.1, 13.1, 16.4
Computers Unlimited – Vectorworks Inc. I 3.1, 18.5, 18.6
HOK I 16.1, 17.2
Keysoft Solutions Ltd. I 16.3, 19.1, 19.2
Mark Bew and Mervyn Richards I 2.1
Martina Miroli (reproduced under Creative Commons license 3.0) I 17.1
McGregor Coxall I 16.2
Patrick MacLeamy I 5.1
Peter Neal I 1.2

PREPARATION

Introduction

Part I of this book provides an overview of Building Information Modelling (BIM) and its key processes, showing some of the many benefits that can be gained from BIM implementation. BIM offers advantages throughout the supply chain – to clients, practices, contractors, suppliers, facilities and landscape managers, and end-users. Clients benefit from improved value, cost control and greater certainty that a project will be delivered on time and within budget. Practices and contractors gain from more efficient project programming, enhanced collaboration, greater transparency, improved decision-making and reduction in rework and delays. Managers and end-users are engaged from the start of a project, leading to a development that is fit for purpose and meets the needs of its users, with an extended handover to ensure that effective maintenance is in place.

How does a practice go about 'implementing BIM'? There is no set way; there are different options for achieving many of the same goals, and different types of practices will take different steps depending on their clients and specialisms. BIM can be implemented in single-handed practices as well as multidisciplinary organisations; a private landscape firm looking to tender for projects in a BIM environment will have a very different BIM implementation process to a local authority seeking to reduce risk and cost to their own projects. One practice might focus on improving information flows and developing better collaborative relationships, whereas another might be looking to bid for new kinds of work and to streamline their processes. The first step whatever the route and destination is to establish the desired outcomes and develop an implementation plan to set the strategy, plan the process and measure the progress. This stage of the BIM journey is covered in Part I.

Starting as a collection of technological tools relating to building construction, BIM is now a process-driven project management system with information at its heart; furthermore, it is now widely applicable beyond the building, to landscape, external works and infrastructure. BIM asks practices to consider their handling of digital information – the means by which it is produced, shared, received and computed – and to find ways to expand, enhance and streamline their information processes.

The built environment sector's relationship with information has not always been associated with innovation, clarity or certainty. The questions that form the basis of this book, and indeed BIM, focus on ways to improve this relationship. What can be done to produce better quality, more reliable project information? How can project teams manage and share information more effectively? Can all project team members and stakeholders receive the information they need, when they need it?

More than this, BIM is about change. This is an undertaking in its own right and whatever the size of the practice or the nature of its work, a managed approach to change, with clarity as to the organisation's strategy, resources, objectives and route, is key. Changes associated with BIM fall into four main categories. First business changes, which affect the running of a practice: being able to offer new services and develop new partnerships, for example. There may be technological changes, in terms of the hardware and software in use within a practice, as well as process changes that mean projects are managed and operated differently. Finally there are team capability changes, as lessons are learnt and new ways of working are explored. The most important element in any change process is people; the way that staff respond to change within the organisation, and their ability and desire to implement that change, is critical. Staff who feel valued will engage positively with change processes, and ongoing training will enable them to implement these changes successfully.

About this book

This book is intended to help landscape and environmental practitioners and those working on landscape projects who are either about to start their BIM journey or have already set out. Rather than providing a prescriptive set of requirements that practitioners must meet, it looks at decisions that will need to be made along the way, offering a roadmap rather than a set route.

Part I focuses on preparation for BIM. It gives an overview of BIM, introducing some organisational prerequisites to BIM implementation, the standards and documentation that govern BIM Level 2, and the roles and responsibilities within a BIM project team. This section is intended to be useful to decision-makers to help identify issues regarding the implications of BIM, and to introduce the essentials of BIM to those just starting out. Part II deals with implementation, showing how BIM processes apply from pre-bid to completion. Part III covers the technological aspects of BIM, addressing the key functionalities of BIM models, software and information processes.

Terminology

The BIM standards use some familiar terms in what may be unfamiliar ways, which will also be used in this book.

- 'Built environment sector' is used to denote the industries that are required to implement BIM Level 2. As of 2016, BIM Level 2 is mandatory for every centrally procured development project in the UK, so this sector includes utilities, construction and transport infrastructure.
- 'Landscape' describes all works that may be within the remit of a landscape project, including built objects and some aspects of infrastructure.

- 'External works' comprises all the works that take place outside the building envelope, including infrastructure, utilities and landscape works.
- 'Asset' and 'facility' refer to the end result of a construction project, which can include landscape features.
- 'Object' denotes a virtual representation of an element or system created with software.
- 'Employer' is used to refer to a party procuring a BIM project.

A glossary at the end of the book defines some of the many acronyms and abbreviations associated with BIM, as well as some BIM-specific terminology.

This book uses the generic term 'practice' throughout to refer to any kind of organisation or business in the private, public or voluntary sector undertaking landscape-related work or shaping landscape policy and strategy, including sole traders, SMEs, multidisciplinary companies, local authorities, voluntary organisations and government agencies. Recognising the diverse range of work undertaken within this array of bodies, the broad term 'landscape practitioners' or 'landscape professionals' is used to cover the spectrum of readers addressed by this book, intended to include landscape architects, landscape planners, landscape managers and urban designers, as well as infrastructure and environmental professionals, specialists, contractors, consultants and all those involved in BIM projects beyond the building.

It is hoped that the information and guidance in this book is shared within project teams and practices, from managers and decision-makers to designers, as well as those responsible for project management, all of whom have a role to play in BIM implementation. Ideally, an understanding of BIM strategy, implementation and the technology that facilitates it will become embedded within a practice seeking to implement BIM Level 2.

There is an aspiration for BIM Level 2 to be exported internationally. The focus of this book is on compliance with current UK regulations, but with an eye to relevance for other regions.

CHAPTER 1

Introduction

This chapter gives a brief introduction to BIM by way of a look at what it is, as well as what it is not, and highlights some of the ways in which landscape practices and clients can gain from adopting BIM processes. The key messages of this book are that BIM can enhance collaboration, streamline information processes, improve decision-making and deliver built environment projects that are fit for purpose and completed on schedule. This chapter and the next begin to outline how.

What is BIM?

The BIM Task Group, set up to help the government's BIM implementation objectives, defines BIM as 'value creating collaboration through the entire life-cycle of an asset, underpinned by the creation, collation and exchange of shared 3D models and intelligent, structured data attached to them' (BIM Task Group, 2013).

The key words in this definition are 'collaboration' and 'data'. BIM is a process, not a technology. Practitioners are not required to work only in 3D, or use particular software. What is required is a willingness to work more collaboratively – delivering a project as a team, rather than as individual practices, with a greater emphasis on shareable digital information and shared models. Collaboration extends beyond the project team, however, and brings in stakeholders such as landscape managers and end-users from the start. A BIM-enabled landscape project begins with the end in mind, delivering not only what is required by the client, but also a landscape that can be maintained and managed effectively, due to the early involvement of those who will be responsible for its maintenance and management after handover.

BIM can mean different things to members of different professions. Within the construction sector, landscape architects, engineers, architects, project managers and contractors, for instance, have all developed their own understandings of BIM, shaped by their particular professional focus and role in the supply chain. For designers and engineers, BIM means working with intelligent design tools to produce data-rich models, whereas project managers and Tier 1 contractors might be more likely to see BIM as a process for reducing risk and waste and improving efficiency (Figure 1.1).

BIM is not software; rather, software is a tool for achieving BIM. A Building Information Model is produced by technology and standardised processes, and implemented by people. Although BIM was portrayed primarily in technological

Figure 1.1
A visualisation based on a Building Information Model

terms in its early days, it is now defined by the 'pillars of BIM', a suite of tools, standards and process documents that set out how BIM is applied throughout the entire life cycle of an asset. These pillars, discussed in detail in Chapter 4, develop an approach to information management that is consistent and transparent, and reduces ambiguity within projects; for instance, regarding the interpretation of drawings or naming strategies.

A practice's BIM maturity is characterised at one of four levels, from 0 to 3. The BIM levels indicate where a practice is on its BIM journey on a spectrum from low collaboration to highly integrated processes amongst the project team. BIM Level 2 is the target set for the construction industry by government, and a requirement for central government-procured projects from 2016. As a result, the built environment sector is bringing its practices into line with the particular requirements of the BIM Level 2 standards – and not just the bare minimum requirements; much work is being done to explore ways of operating projects that further improve collaboration and reduce conflict, including contractual and insurance provisions.

It is worth noting that the requirements of a BIM Level 2 project are not necessarily significantly different from those of traditional projects. London's Queen Elizabeth Olympic Park is a recent example (Figure 1.2). Although not officially a 'BIM project', it demonstrated all the key attributes of BIM Level 2, particularly in regard to collaboration. Each consultant used a combination of software to generate drawings and models to defined standards, which were published to a shared environment, and incorporated into federated models, supported by 3D where appropriate. This

process is not uncommon and BIM is in effect an evolution of existing principles of collaboration. What is new is that BIM is governed by better defined processes, to new and emerging standards with a greater level of rigour regarding deliverables, and a new clarity as to the roles and requirements for the development and management of information.

Figure 1.2 The Queen Elizabeth Olympic Park: effective collaboration is at the heart of a project that truly delivers its potential

Why do BIM?

The goals of BIM in the UK are:

> Significant improvement in cost, value and carbon performance . . . achieved through the use of open shareable asset information . . . helping the supply chain unlock more efficient and collaborative ways of work throughout the entire project and asset life-cycle end to end.
>
> (BIM Task Group, 2013)

('Asset' in this context can refer to a built environment project in its entirety, or to its component parts: from a whole building at one end of the scale, to its paving and planting at the other.)

BIM provides a managed approach to the execution of built environment projects that integrates technological benefits into a standardised practice, with increased certainty as to how a project operates, greater transparency, and clarity of responsibility and activity. BIM Level 2 does not rewrite how projects operate; rather, it coordinates collaboration, and structures the activities of data exchange into a planned process. Coordination of the project from the outset supports landscape architects in their responsibility to create spaces that are constructible, maintainable and cost-effective. The result of a successful collaborative process is a landscape that is right first time, fulfilling the needs of the client and serving the users.

BIM is a means of improving decision-making in the construction and management of built environment projects, increasing the quality of information available to the project team and stakeholders. Structured collaboration reduces the rework and delays that can hamper the planning and delivery of projects. Simulation of the design throughout its development helps make a project's programme and costs more predictable from early on. In particular, one of the main benefits cited by employers – in BIM, those procuring landscapes and built assets – is a reduction in cost and time uncertainty in construction. Furthermore, the lifetime costs of an asset can also be reduced by ensuring that the project meets the needs of users after handover, and by providing information to use in adaptation to any required future changes.

The landscape profession provides a crucial connection between the need to manage the landscape and its character, and the need for development. The 2016 BIM mandate on government projects requires landscape practitioners to demonstrate that they are capable of operating in a BIM Level 2 project environment in order to work on centrally procured projects. BIM implementation has already gained momentum amongst first tier contractors, who are increasingly mandating the use of BIM on their projects. It is therefore vital that the landscape and environmental professions embrace BIM in order to continue their essential involvement on built environment projects.

The following chapters set out the preparatory stages for BIM implementation within landscape practices, beginning with the thinking behind BIM and an introduction to the main tools, standards and processes involved. Organisational issues including staff development and relationships with clients and partners are then considered in light of the changes to a practice that BIM can bring about. This preparation leads up to the BIM Implementation Plan, covered in the final chapter of Part I. As the key planning tool for the BIM journey, it sets out how the practice puts in place everything that is needed to begin working on BIM Level 2 projects.

Reference

BIM Task Group (2013) *Frequently asked questions*. London: Department for Business, Innovation and Skills. www.bimtaskgroup.org/bim-faqs/

CHAPTER 2

Understanding BIM

Introduction

This chapter starts by looking at BIM Levels 0 to 3 as a framework for understanding the processes and scope of BIM engagement. It shows how BIM workflows differ from traditional processes and the cost benefits that BIM offers. After outlining the origins of BIM for historical context and the management schools of thought that have shaped its development, there is an overview of the UK's BIM implementation strategy, considered as part of the government's wider strategic objectives relating to sustainability, competitiveness and cost-effectiveness in the construction industry.

BIM levels

BIM Levels 0 to 3 provide a notional scale indicating the level of BIM adoption within a practice. The BIM wedge, or Bew–Richards Maturity Model (Figure 2.1), named after Mervyn Richards and Mark Bew who developed it, clearly illustrates the levels in a way that enables practices to identify where they are on their BIM journey. The bars below the wedge indicate, possibly less clearly, a number of standards that could or should be a part of BIM implementation. BIM Level 2 is the target set for the construction industry by the Government Construction Strategy (Cabinet Office, 2011). As an illustrative model, the BIM wedge does not provide formal validation of BIM maturity; Levels 0, 1 and 3 do not have a process in place for their assessment or implementation and are indicative levels only:

- *BIM Level 0*
  Unmanaged Computer Aided Design (CAD) in 2D: information is exchanged between project participants in flat, uneditable documents, either printed or digital files such as PDFs.
- *BIM Level 1*
  Also known as 'lonely BIM': managed CAD in 2D or 3D, using BS 1192:2007 (BSI, 2007) to describe project roles and file-naming strategy. A cloud-based collaboration tool acts as the Common Data Environment (CDE) for project models. There are some standards for data structures and formats. Commercial data is managed by stand-alone finance and cost management packages with no integration.

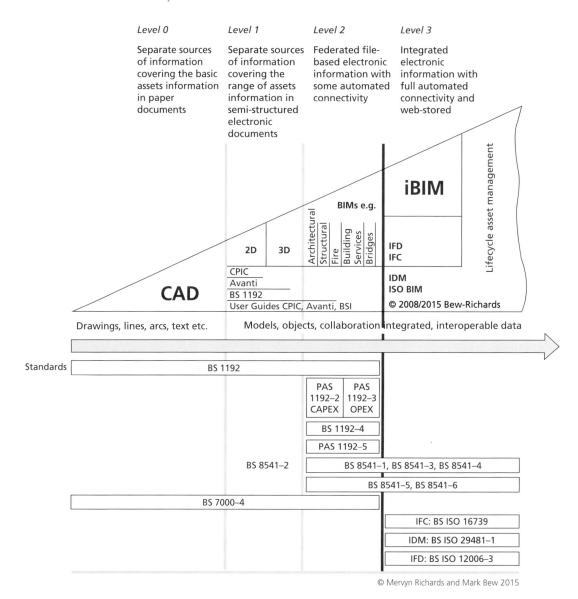

Level 0

Separate sources of information covering the basic assets information in paper documents

Level 1

Separate sources of information covering the range of assets information in semi-structured electronic documents

Level 2

Federated file-based electronic information with some automated connectivity

Level 3

Integrated electronic information with full automated connectivity and web-stored

© 2008/2015 Bew-Richards

© Mervyn Richards and Mark Bew 2015

Figure 2.1 The Bew–Richards BIM Maturity Model, commonly known as the BIM wedge

- *BIM Level 2*

  A managed 3D environment held in separate discipline BIM tools with attached data. Commercial data is managed by an enterprise resource planner or other business process management system. Integrated information is provided by the project team using a combination of file formats and software tools. Time planning and cost planning may also feature within the systems used on the project.

- *BIM Level 3*

  BIM Level 3 is undergoing development as part of the Digital Built Britain strategy. At the time of writing, this envisages a single model that each member of the project team can access and model within. This fully open process and data integration is to be enabled by the IFC (Industry Foundation Classes) file format and the IFD (International Framework for Dictionaries) terminology standard. Project information will be managed by a collaborative model server.

The model demonstrates a path along which practices can progress in order to develop their BIM capabilities, vital to ensuring internal buy-in to improvements in processes and technology. It illustrates that the use of geometry tools alone is insufficient to claim BIM Level 2 maturity; at the higher levels, model information is delivered in 3D with a greater depth of information. Along with these data-rich models, the British Standards and others referenced in the BIM wedge create a codified information management structure that enables digital information to be shared across disciplines.

Overview of a BIM Level 2 project

This section gives a brief introduction to processes within a BIM Level 2 project where they differ from traditional processes; all the stages are described in more detail in subsequent chapters. The main distinguishing feature of BIM Level 2 is the focus on the role of information. The project work stages do not change, and the overall process of developing a built asset remains the same. However, improved collaboration using shareable data enables a more streamlined design and development process, with greater transparency.

The pillars of BIM provide the core standards for Level 2. They relate mainly to information management, and are supplemented by standard project documents created by the employer's team and the project team which set out the collaborative processes that they will follow. This information management structure gives employers, consultants, the supply chain and stakeholders a new degree of certainty about a project, providing a more stable platform to the development and improving decision-making processes. By the time construction begins, much of the work has in fact already been done; the project is developed as a digital model, allowing issues that require redesign or rework to be resolved before work on site begins.

Looking at the BIM Level 2 timeline step-by-step, the process begins with the employer preparing and issuing an Employer's Information Requirements (EIR) document, developed from a set of plain language questions (PLQs) as part of the tendering process (Figure 2.2). The EIR sets out the employer's specific technological and process management requirements for the project. A bidding team responds with their BIM Execution Plan (BEP), proposing their approach to the brief and describing their BIM competencies. The relationship between these key documents creates a line of continuity throughout the project from the start.

The appointed team then submits a post-contract award BEP detailing how they will deliver the project, which will go on to form contractual requirements. Stakeholders undertake a pre-commencement process to plan the best use of information exchanges, making sure that information deliverables are relevant not only to the employer and the project team, but also to maintenance and future works. After commencement, the EIR is reviewed at the start of each project stage and the BEP amended as needed in light of the project's development. An ongoing lessons-learnt process reviews knowledge gained by the employer and the project team, and identifies successes and failures.

Inception, Brief and Commencement

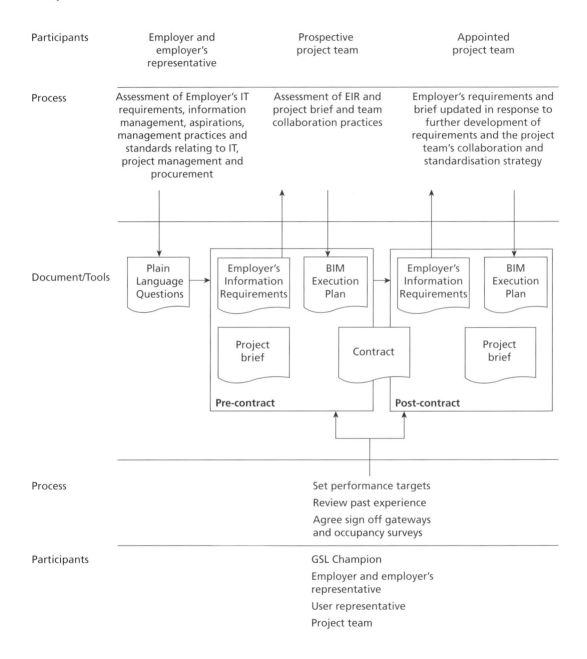

Participants	Employer and employer's representative	Prospective project team	Appointed project team
Process	Assessment of Employer's IT requirements, information management, aspirations, management practices and standards relating to IT, project management and procurement	Assessment of EIR and project brief and team collaboration practices	Employer's requirements and brief updated in response to further development of requirements and the project team's collaboration and standardisation strategy

Document/Tools:

Plain Language Questions → Employer's Information Requirements → BIM Execution Plan → Employer's Information Requirements — BIM Execution Plan

Project brief — Contract — Project brief

Pre-contract   **Post-contract**

Process	Set performance targets
	Review past experience
	Agree sign off gateways and occupancy surveys

Participants	GSL Champion
	Employer and employer's representative
	User representative
	Project team

Figure 2.2 Inception, brief and commencement phase: processes ensure that the project has clear protocols from the start

BIM creates some new roles to manage project information effectively. A key role is the Information Manager, responsible for defining how information is managed on the project, and maintaining the Common Data Environment (CDE), a remote secure storage system that acts as the central repository for information files during the project. Before upload to the CDE, files are given a simple suitability code

Design and Construction

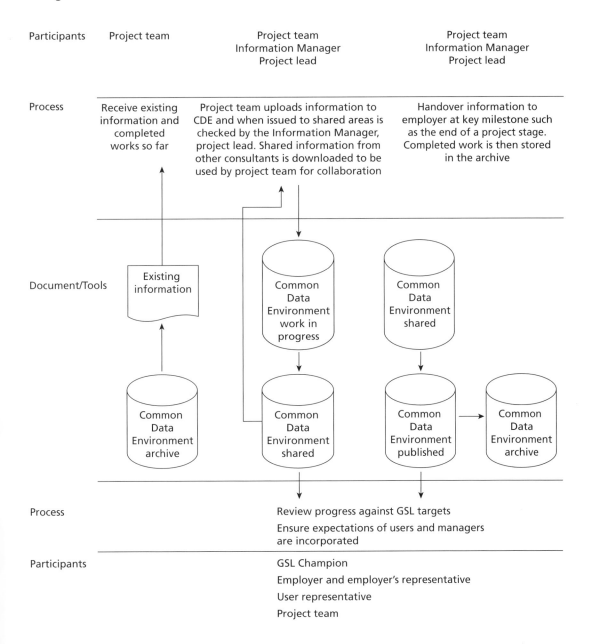

Participants	Project team	Project team Information Manager Project lead	Project team Information Manager Project lead
Process	Receive existing information and completed works so far	Project team uploads information to CDE and when issued to shared areas is checked by the Information Manager, project lead. Shared information from other consultants is downloaded to be used by project team for collaboration	Handover information to employer at key milestone such as the end of a project stage. Completed work is then stored in the archive

Document/Tools

- Existing information
- Common Data Environment work in progress
- Common Data Environment shared
- Common Data Environment archive
- Common Data Environment shared
- Common Data Environment published
- Common Data Environment archive

Process

Review progress against GSL targets

Ensure expectations of users and managers are incorporated

Participants

GSL Champion

Employer and employer's representative

User representative

Project team

defining the extent to which the information they contain can be relied on, so that during the project all parties can ensure that they are providing correct information for others to use, and using the correct information themselves, avoiding coordination errors (Figure 2.3).

At the end of each project stage, or as defined within the EIR, information is moved from the working area of the CDE into an area designated for published files.

Figure 2.3 Design and construction phase: working with a Common Data Environment gives a project a high level of transparency

This is an official handover of information to the employer, known as a data drop. The employer, together with the procurement and management team, devises a set of plain language questions to ask at each data drop, setting out the requirements of each stage in unambiguous terms. Each data drop should allow those questions to be answered.

Once the construction phase is complete, the handover phase commences. This is a comprehensive process in BIM Level 2, thanks to Government Soft Landings (GSL). A GSL Champion or lead facilitator, independent of the employer and the project team, will liaise with all parties throughout the project to check that the ongoing

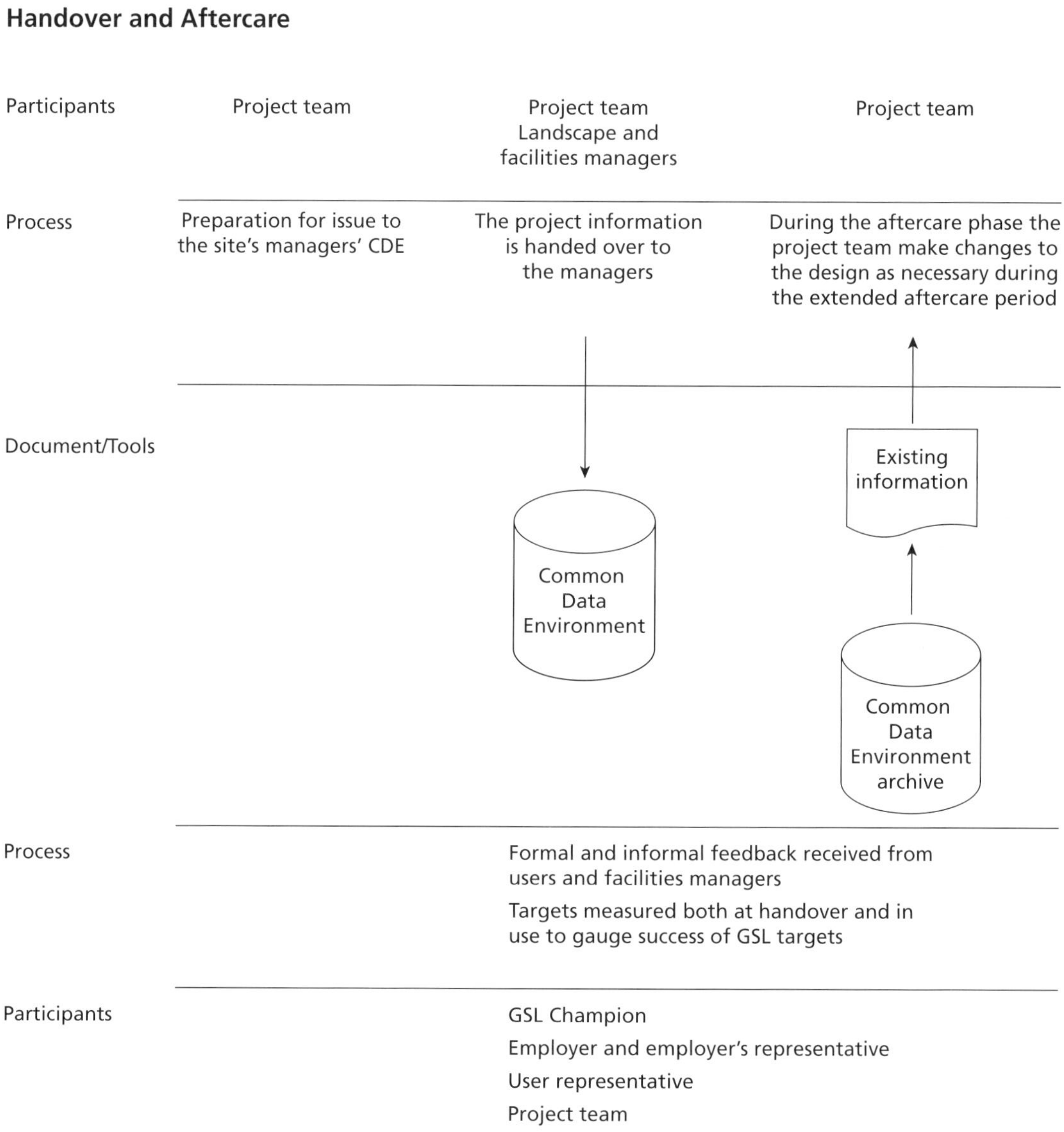

Figure 2.4 Handover and aftercare phase: issuing the CDE to the managers of the site is not the end of the project

Handover and Aftercare

| Participants | Project team | Project team
Landscape and
facilities managers | Project team |
|---|---|---|---|
| Process | Preparation for issue to the site's managers' CDE | The project information is handed over to the managers | During the aftercare phase the project team make changes to the design as necessary during the extended aftercare period |
| Document/Tools | | Common Data Environment | Existing information / Common Data Environment archive |
| Process | | Formal and informal feedback received from users and facilities managers
Targets measured both at handover and in use to gauge success of GSL targets | |
| Participants | | GSL Champion
Employer and employer's representative
User representative
Project team | |

work reflects the employer's and users' requirements. The asset's managers and users have greater scope to give their input during development, and feedback once it is in use. The asset may operate as designed, but more than this, it must operate as users require. The project team is obliged to make adjustments when needed, requiring retention of design and construction teams for a longer period post-completion.

The final stage is the project team handover of the deliverables to the employer's team (Figure 2.4). The EIR determines the relevant information to hand over, facilitated by the GSL Champion, making sure that the outputs will work with the software used in managing the asset and enabling the facilities and landscape managers to understand the elements and products on site. A key feature of a BIM Level 2 project is the legacy of high-quality information handed over at completion to inform any future refurbishment or development.

Where do the savings come from?

BIM offers significant value to an employer throughout the project life cycle in many ways, for instance:

- better integrated design leads to lower construction costs, through less waste and fewer changes on site;
- more reliable information on scheduling avoids delays and consequent spiralling fees;
- improved risk management realises savings at a strategic level.

Last but not least, the most considerable potential for savings comes from the employer's and managers' better understanding of the asset before handover and its operation in use. The greatest costs of a landscape arise during its operational lifetime, far exceeding those of the design and construction phase. BIM enables a better understanding of these costs.

An employer should not, however, expect every cost to be lower on a BIM project; BIM is about quality enhancement as well as cost savings. BIM enables employers to make better decisions, based on better quality information, and improved information quality permeates throughout the project life cycle. Employers who remember the maxim that £1 spent on design saves £10 in construction and £100 in operation, and who recognise greater predictability as part of a project's value for money, will appreciate what BIM offers. Clients who only look at the bottom line design fees will miss out on the wider cost and programme benefits to be had throughout the life cycle of a project.

Origins of BIM

The term 'Building Information Modelling' first appeared in print in 1992 (van Nederveen and Tolman, 1992). The concept of BIM software first emerged in the 1970s, however, in an article by Chuck Eastman entitled 'The use of computers instead of drawings in building design' (Eastman, 1975). BIM has been walking the line between 2D drawings and 3D modelling ever since its inception and it is still standard practice for BIM processes to include both forms of information production.

Eastman's seminal article also considered the use of databases within the design process, another core BIM concept. CAD applications are essentially databases of object types, with location and geometry defined by coordinates. BIM allows extended structured data to describe these objects, enabling the creation of a virtual construction object, and making a wealth of analyses possible. Realistic representation is a continuing aspiration of the BIM community and every new generation of software brings the industry closer to achieving it.

BIM has gradually spread around the world with a number of countries developing their own BIM approach, whether mandated by government or led by industry. BIM in the UK draws on two schools of thought: one focusing on the power of technology, the other following lean construction. Both seek to address the same issues within the built environment industry, although the exterior design industries' path towards BIM has arguably been less technology-focused.

The technology school

The technology school of thought seeks more powerful and versatile tools to create virtual objects, with the emphasis on finding technical solutions to problems (while, it is hoped, heeding Bill Gates' words: 'The first rule of any technology used in a business is that automation applied to an efficient operation will magnify the efficiency. The second is that automation applied to an inefficient operation will magnify the inefficiency.').

The technological aspects of BIM have not developed in isolation and many of its benefits are associated with wider digital trends across other sectors. Increased computer processing power, for instance, has facilitated the development of more powerful software that can perform increasingly complex tasks. The open source movement, advanced simulation, the internet, computer graphics and improved sensing have all played a part in the technological evolution of BIM.

The open source movement champions free information sharing, whereby contributors develop and adapt a system or software; the IFC and OpenBIM information exchange formats are products of open source, allowing consultants on a project to share information produced on different software platforms. Increased processing power has enabled advanced simulation, which has been harnessed extensively in the manufacturing sector in prototyping designs. This has created an increased appetite for simulation within other sectors, with the built environment sector now using the technology to model the use of spaces, their energy consumption and microclimates, for instance.

At the same time, computer graphics have advanced in complexity and nuance, resulting in the challenge to produce more and more realistic or imaginative visualisations of built environment schemes. A new generation of web-based communications technology enables information sharing at ever-higher speeds, which together with cloud computing allows consultants in different sectors to work remotely as a team on the same files. Finally, sensing, in terms of laser scanning and point cloud capture, allows hyper-realistic surveys that can model the environment with great accuracy, facilitating modelling and design work in a digital environment that closely mimics real-world conditions.

These technological advances have led to the production of hardware and software tools able to produce digital assets that increasingly represent the landscape as it will be constructed and used. These have not been linear developments, however, and the individual software tools that serve different professions continue to evolve at different speeds. The result is a technological landscape varying in maturity, necessitating the development of standardised processes and planning methodologies that the BIM Level 2 standards have developed from lean construction.

The lean school

Lean construction is the underpinning rationale of BIM Level 2 and is embedded within the UK Government Construction Strategy. The lean approach to process management, also known as Just in Time (JIT) management, originated in vehicle manufacturing at Toyota and has been adopted in many other sectors. Key lean concepts for BIM are 'value' and 'waste'. Activities and materials that do not contribute to the project outcomes, or over-deliver, are termed waste; activities and materials for which the client is willing to pay are deemed of value – and everything that is not of value is waste. According to lean, forms of waste that can be found in built environment design processes are:

- *Defects*: flawed designs can have a knock-on effect throughout a project, causing costs to spiral, especially if only detected once construction has begun.
- *Overproduction*: creating a more advanced design than is necessary for the project stage would be considered overproducing, for example.
- *Waiting*: given the complex dependencies within construction design, waiting for the completion of dependent tasks can be particularly detrimental to project timelines – and costly, due to standing time.
- *Not utilising talent*: making effective use of the talent within an organisation is a prime lean strategy for waste reduction.
- *Transport waste*: eliminating unnecessary movement saves time and costs, whether it is people, physical materials or data being moved.
- *Inventory waste*: large numbers of documents remaining as work-in-progress, for instance, can be considered waste inventory.
- *Motion waste*: this was identified at Toyota in the classic tale of a box of bolts being moved from the end of a workbench and placed next to the operatives who used them; a document control methodology that reduces time spent searching for information is a BIM parallel.
- *Excess processing*: completing a job in twenty steps that could have been done in ten is excess processing; this could include, for example, awkward strategies to import another consultant's work, or manually adjusting designs for spatial coordination.

BIM in the UK

The built environment industry has long been a source of concern to UK governments. Successive public reports have identified failings within the sector, from the

Simon Report's findings on efficiency (Ministry of Works, 1944), to segregation into professional silos in the Emmerson Report (Ministry of Works, 1962) and the Banwell Report (Ministry of Public Building and Works, 1964). Government-commissioned reports in more recent times continue to find wastefulness, ineffective processes and fragmentation resulting in ongoing underperformance and poor value for money (see, e.g., Latham, 1994; Egan, 1998; Wolstenholme et al., 2009).

This underperformance provides the backdrop to BIM in the UK. The Task Force that produced the Egan Report included representatives from sectors such as supermarkets and car manufacturers, from whom it was felt the construction industry could learn. The resulting shift towards lean construction, embodied in the current BIM strategy, relies heavily on lean manufacturing as its intellectual underpinning.

Government Construction Strategy

Under the Government Construction Strategy, 'the Government will require fully collaborative 3D BIM (with all project and asset information, documentation and data being electronic) as a minimum' (Cabinet Office, 2011: 14). Besides the BIM requirement, it presents a number of other objectives for the industry, namely:

- value for money and the approach to value for money
- efficiency and elimination of waste
- alignment of design and construction with operation and asset management
- supplier relationship management
- competitiveness and reducing duplication
- new procurement models
- client relationship management
- implementation of existing and emerging government policy in relation to sustainability and carbon

It is worth remembering these other requirements in planning BIM implementation. The BIM Task Group, set up to help deliver the government's BIM implementation objectives, gave its BIM strategy paper the strapline 'Management for value, cost and carbon improvement' (BIM Industry Working Group, 2011), highlighting that BIM also addresses the construction strategy's other aims. BIM is therefore not just a target to be met, but also an innovation tool to address many of the government's sector-wide requirements.

References

BIM Industry Working Group (2011) *BIM: Management for value, cost and carbon improvement, a report for the Government Construction Client Group.* London: Department of Business Innovation and Skills.

BSI (2007) *BS 1192:2007: Collaborative production of architectural, engineering and construction information. Code of practice.* London: British Standards Institution.

Cabinet Office (2011) *Government construction strategy.* London: Cabinet Office.

Eastman, C.M. (1975) The use of computers instead of drawings in building design. *AIA Journal,* 63(3): 46–50.

Egan, J. (1998) *Rethinking construction: Report of the Construction Task Force.* London: HMSO.

Latham, M. (1994) *Constructing the team.* London: HMSO.

Ministry of Public Building and Works (1964) *The placing and management of contracts for building and civil engineering work* (Banwell Report). London: HMSO.

Ministry of Works (1944) *Report of the Committee on the Placing and Management of Building Contracts* (Simon Report). London: HMSO.

Ministry of Works (1962) *Survey of problems before the construction industries* (Emmerson Report). London: HMSO.

van Nederveen, G.A. and Tolman, F. (1992) Modelling multiple views on buildings. *Automation in Construction,* 1(3): 215–224.

Wolstenholme, A. et al. (2009) *Never waste a good crisis: A review of progress since Rethinking Construction and thoughts for our future.* London: Constructing Excellence.

CHAPTER 3

Prerequisites

Introduction

The BIM journey requires few prerequisites; all that is needed is the capacity and willingness to change within a practice, a good network of co-consultants who are keen to reap the benefits of collaboration, and clients who want to see work done more effectively. This chapter covers some of the organisational and practical first steps to BIM implementation, including a look at some of the drivers for change, a review of business culture and processes within the practice, software considerations, staff development and training.

Drivers for change

Whether looking to keep up with competitors or win new kinds of work, a practice that fosters professional development and values knowledge-sharing will adapt much more readily to BIM processes. The decision to implement BIM may be a logical next step within current strategic objectives; it may come from the desire to build on the skills of existing staff and design partners, or it may be driven by the aspirations of clients – or the types of work the practice aspires to undertake in the future. There is also the momentum created by an evolving sector and the practices that are adapting to the new environment. Those who want to work with them need to adapt too; those who do not adapt may well be left behind.

In addition to a review of organisational culture and staff capacity, a practice could consider some operational issues in the planning phase. For instance, internal plans of work and processes can be analysed to identify BIM opportunities and obstacles, current quality assurance arrangements can be checked to see where BIM fits and complies, and IT capacity can be reviewed. This is also the time to start conversations with clients and partners to begin planning BIM methodology.

Software

BIM is not software, and there is no out-of-the-box, one-size-fits-all BIM package. A practice may decide to purchase new software as a result of the BIM implementation process, but this should not be the first step.

Before purchasing any software, a practice should analyse both its own requirements and those of relevant teams, partners, clients and other stakeholders to gain an understanding of the functionality required. Software decisions should reflect the processes by which information will be shared on BIM projects within teams; the requirement for information that is shareable and usable by the wider team should inform key decisions for BIM implementation later on in the process. Every project team member, whether in landscape, engineering, architecture or facilities management, should be free to choose their own software, notwithstanding the necessity to comply with the recognised standards for sharing the information created.

There are also questions to ask of existing software at the start of the BIM journey. Collaboration, design and analysis software are the broad categories most frequently used in landscape and related work, and some specific issues for each type are suggested below. There are also common criteria to consider, such as efficiency, cost, reliability and interoperability.

Collaboration software

A collaborative project environment has some specific requirements:

- *Compliance with standards*: BIM Level 2 standards require the use of certain naming conventions, with which a collaboration tool will need to work.
- *Accountability and transparency*: the ability to track the use of information by the project team is important in helping maintain a culture of openness on the project.
- *Security from attack*: online construction collaboration solutions must be well protected given the sensitivity of the information that they may hold.
- *Retention*: the length of time that files can be stored may determine whether or not a collaboration solution is suitable.
- *Version control*: handling versions of documents, data and models is a vital aspect of information management.

Design tools

At the heart of BIM tools is the ability to generate information from geometry and vice versa. The connection between geometry and information offered by a software package can be seen in the steps required to make changes to designs and in the software's ability to respond automatically to new information or geometry. For example, changing the density of plants in a planting bed should increase the overall number of plants in the design. Design software should be assessed in terms of how it creates and shares information; it may actually be fit for purpose already. It should also be considered in terms of information exchanges with other software packages, for purposes such as clash detection, spatial coordination, analysis and issue (discussed in more detail in Chapter 8). There is a variety of software in use throughout the sector, so information exchange requirements will need to be considered in terms of the purposes of sharing, together with the practice's BIM Implementation Plan.

Analysis tools

It will be helpful to consider the types of analysis that will be performed, the data that
are required, and how these will be supplied. Types of analysis include analysing mapping, specification, sustainability or costing information, providing insights that data
in isolation cannot. Each of these tasks has different information requirements and
will require data to be provided in a format that is usable by the tools in place. When
analysing a landscape in terms of its capacity for new wind turbines, for example, it
is useful to be able to assess the Zone of Visual Influence with analysis tools that can
use mapping data and generate 3D topography from this information (Figure 3.1).

Assessment process

Much can be learnt from considering the results of a software assessment with frequent clients and collaborators. Small recurring problems can be thrown into sharp
relief and may be seen to add up to larger and costly inefficiencies. It will be useful to
do this assessment with the professions with which the most work is done, and to ask
of each other 'What information do you need?' Rework costs time and money, and
reducing it is in everyone's interests. Information carriers such as objects or files can
create the need for rework, and it is worth asking collaborators about information that
is often missing or has to be resubmitted, requiring the re-entering of 3D points for
topography or the redrawing of a 3D object, for instance. This approach improves the
chances of BIM implementation leading to cost savings for practices and employers.

The use and function of software does not suddenly change with BIM. An appropriate software strategy should be based on an assessment of existing software
practices and those of important collaborators and clients. Some criteria to assess
the current software mix and potential future purchases against might be:

• *Performance requirements*: what tasks must be performed on BIM projects?
• *Interoperability*: to what extent can information be shared with other software?

- *Hardware requirements*: what hardware specifications are necessary to run the software?
- *Software requirements*: are supporting software products or plug-ins needed?
- *Network requirements*: what connection speed and reliability is required? (This can be an issue for rural practices and those who depend on mobile devices.)
- *Licensing requirements*: are individual licences required or network licensing? Can software be used simultaneously on different machines?
- *Training requirements*: how much staff training is needed? Will all staff need training to the same level?
- *Changes to internal standards and processes*: file-handling protocols will need to conform to BIM standards, and software will need to handle this.
- *Software support*: what is required of those providing software support in-house, and what external support by the software developer or other third parties is necessary?

Training

Just as the move from paper to CAD required training and changes in landscape practices' work processes, so too does BIM implementation. Staff who are willing and able to develop are essential to the change process. The Chartership syllabus for landscape professionals now requires an understanding of BIM, and this will develop as BIM implementation evolves. Landscape professionals are required to undertake CPD (Continuing Professional Development) as part of a commitment to lifelong learning and the upholding of professional standards, presenting an ideal opportunity to develop and maintain BIM knowledge.

Although it should be reiterated that BIM is not software, and buying software should not be the first step of the BIM journey, software training should nonetheless be considered a prerequisite for BIM implementation. Software competence is invaluable. A discussion with current software suppliers about the BIM benefits offered by their products can be a useful starting point, helping assess the potential for implementing BIM within a practice, as well as identifying training needs. It is worth analysing the desired outcomes of BIM training, for individuals and the project team, and identifying specific gains that can be applied to future projects. Software training for BIM should be incorporated into existing training practices and the overall business strategy, and should qualify as accredited CPD.

It is important to select expert guidance appropriate to a practice's needs and those of the sector; trainers experienced in landscape will not only benefit those working at the design end, but also have a beneficial effect downstream for contractors and maintenance staff, who need to be able to engage with the information they will receive. Training is considered as part of the BIM Implementation Plan, the formal methodology for BIM adoption within a practice, in Chapter 7.

Qualifications

Strictly speaking, BIM qualifications are not a prerequisite. However, practices looking to buy in expertise or hire new staff to take their BIM adoption forward may consider qualifications essential. Employers interviewing new staff for BIM roles may find it helpful to remember the words attributed to Albert Einstein: 'If you can't explain it simply, you don't understand it well enough.'

Software-specific qualifications exist, but the ability to develop new software techniques or refine existing ones will also be of value in enabling the project team to work more collaboratively and innovatively. Perhaps unsurprisingly, official qualification as a BIM expert is viewed with some suspicion by the industry's current BIM experts. Nevertheless, the range of qualifications is increasing, and BIM features to varying extents on existing landscape degree courses. At the time of writing, there is no formal qualification for BIM in landscape in the UK. Qualifications in BIM are offered by universities and professional organisations, and can be awarded either to individuals or companies.

In a practice's early stages of BIM adoption, individuals with a willingness to learn and the scope to learn on the job should be sufficient to deliver progress. A qualification is only worth the weight given to it by clients and the industry, and the relative weight of currently available qualifications is in flux. However, as more experienced BIM practitioners take up positions of leadership within practices, more qualifications are likely to be required of new entrants or project team members.

University-based qualifications

University qualifications cover the conceptual underpinning of BIM, but will not necessarily provide practical experience in the use of BIM technologies and processes. Those looking to specialise in the external works field may need to have used opportunities such as a dissertation or placement in order to develop their knowledge beyond lean construction and BIM for buildings. For employers, a narrow range of experience may be offset by the breadth and depth of knowledge graduates can bring, from which practices can develop potential methodologies for developing BIM implementation.

Professional organisations

A number of organisations provide BIM Level 2 training. The BRE (Building Research Establishment) offers a course to become a BIM-accredited professional, and a BIM Level 2 certification scheme for businesses. Current assessment of competency is based on completion of documents that project teams must work with, and there is an annual charge and assessment process for this service.

Further support

A network of free support and guidance exists within BIM4, Constructing Excellence and BIM Hubs. These volunteer-based organisations have wide experience and a good understanding of how professional practices are engaging with BIM, which can help those setting out on their BIM journey to clarify their plans.

CHAPTER 4

Documents

Introduction

Having considered some of the internal issues and drivers for a practice moving to BIM implementation, this chapter turns to the 'pillars of BIM', the standard documents that govern BIM Level 2 and structure its processes. It also looks at some of the project-specific documents that are required.

BIM Level 2 standardises the processes and timings of projects, and successful implementation involves understanding the obligations that this places upon the project team. A BIM Level 2 project requires extra preparation and planning, and the creation, review and approval of a suite of documents. This is intended to ensure that every project stakeholder has a clear understanding of the work that will be done – when, how and by whom. BIM offers an alternative in this regard to some of the inefficiencies of traditional information processes, with clients likely to receive project documentation at practical completion containing inaccuracies, inconsistencies, duplications and omissions.

Two types of document are associated with BIM Level 2: guidance documents and project documents. The pillars of BIM are the guidance documents, providing the supporting structure of every BIM Level 2 project and any practice's BIM implementation process. Project-specific documents are then developed around this structure, dealing with both the broad approach to technology and project management, and the granular detail of information-sharing processes.

In the UK, the British Standards Institution has created the project standards for BIM Level 2. The guidance documents may be followed to the letter, and this book will not advise otherwise, but it is worth noting that some parallel processes and terminologies have emerged reflecting BIM's evolution in various directions around the world and implementation within different professions. Some leading BIM practitioners have adapted naming conventions, classification systems and forms, for example, so that the project roles set out in PAS 1192-2:2013 (BSI, 2013) are sometimes termed 'BIM superuser' or 'BIM champion'. Ultimately, high-quality BIM implementation is achieved through communication and collaboration, and agreeing a path that benefits all parties.

The pillars of BIM

The British Standards and other resources that comprise the pillars of BIM are continually evolving and will continue to do so (Figure 4.1). The pillars detailed here were in force at the time of writing, but will change. For example, BS ISO 19650 is set to replace PAS 1192-2:2013, and may also integrate other standards and specifications listed here. It is therefore essential to check the currency of standards and tools to ensure that the correct versions are used on a project, and to be aware of any changes due.

CIC BIM Protocol

The Construction Industry Council BIM Protocol (CIC, 2013) is intended to provide the legal underpinning of a BIM Level 2 project, forming the basis for additional clauses within the project team's contracts. It defines the requirements and outlines the method of delivery for project information. The main body of the document relates to key legal aspects, defining where responsibilities lie, and identifying matters of intellectual property, such as permitted uses, liability, change management and ownership. It also defines the role of the Information Manager (see Chapter 6) and steps to ensure the effectiveness of this role. The BIM Protocol has two appendices, which cover project-specific matters. They require a definition of the project's information requirements and the completion of a responsibilities matrix for information production, showing who will be producing the information.

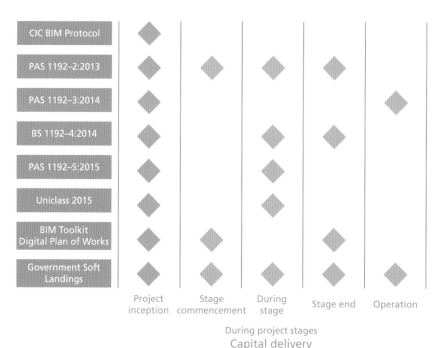

Figure 4.1 The pillars of BIM support the process of implementing BIM on a project; their use should be planned carefully to ensure that they deliver their full potential

BS 1192:2007: Collaborative production of architectural, engineering and construction information

This standard (BSI, 2007) is the foundation stone of BIM Level 2 and is referenced directly or indirectly by the other standards listed here. It sets out the new roles required to manage BIM Level 2 and their responsibilities. It also covers the CDE, defining how information is managed, and the Standard Methods and Procedures, defining how objects are named and organised. BS 1192:2007 was under review at the time of writing.

PAS 1192-2:2013: Specification for information management for the capital/delivery phase of assets using Building Information Modelling

PAS 1192-2:2013 (BSI, 2013) provides the project management guidebook for BIM Level 2 project delivery. It details all the roles and responsibilities of those involved in the design and construction phase, and also applies BS 1192:2007 to the project timeline with its stages.

BS 1192-4:2014: Collaborative production of information. Part 4: Fulfilling employers' information exchange requirements using COBie – Code of practice

COBie (Construction Operations Building information exchange) provides an information exchange mechanism for the delivery of information across the life cycle of the asset. The COBie code of practice (BSI, 2014b) defines a methodology for the transfer of information that allows employers, asset managers and facility managers to define their expectations, and enables information providers, including the lead designers and contractors, to prepare accessible information. COBie is discussed in more detail in Chapter 18.

PAS 1192-5:2015: Specification for security-minded building information modelling, digital built environments and smart asset management

This document (BSI, 2015) outlines the potential security issues present within a built environment project so that all parties can operate in a security-conscious manner.

PAS 1192-3:2014: Specification for information management for the operational phase of assets using Building Information Modelling

This document (BSI, 2014a) ensures that accurate, complete and unambiguous information is transferred to the asset's managers and operation team at handover, and sets out how that information should be maintained and used throughout the life cycle of the asset.

Government Soft Landings (GSL)

GSL consists of a suite of documents available from the BIM Task Group website (Government Soft Landings, 2013). They define a new form of handover process that involves the facilities management and operational management team, as well as the users of the asset. GSL is intended to enable a smoother transition into an asset's operational phase, through the involvement of the design and construction teams beyond practical completion.

The BIM Toolkit/Digital Plan of Works

This pillar is a free, government-sponsored web-based resource (NBS, 2015a). It works in conjunction with the project documents to provide the single point of truth regarding responsibilities and timings. Along with a collection of project management tools, the Toolkit contains two other pillars of BIM: a Digital Plan of Works (DPoW) and a classification system, Uniclass 2015.

    The DPoW is used in conjunction with project management tools to produce the Model Production and Delivery Table (MPDT) which should be used as Appendix 1 of the BIM Protocol to define the responsibilities for modelling and Level of Detail required for deliverables (see Chapter 19 for more on Level of Detail).

Uniclass 2015

Uniclass 2015 (NBS, 2015b) provides a unified construction industry classification system that allows a common means for organising much of the information on a construction project. It enables a wide range of objects in a project to be classified, from the type of facility being built, down to the individual components of products, across landscape, buildings, engineering and infrastructure. This system is used in project management to categorise project information.

Project documents

A number of project documents exist within the life of a BIM Level 2 project, detailing specific information responsibilities and processes. This section gives an overview of the part these documents play in the process of design and construction; further detail is provided in Chapter 11 on their implementation on a project. The two key project documents are the EIR, produced by the employer, and the BEP, produced by the project team.

    Project documents evolve through three different stages. They start life at the assessment stage, when the capacity to work in a BIM environment, the human resource provisions and the IT capabilities are considered. At the implementation stage, they set out a methodology and practice for the project duration when it has been agreed what will be delivered, along with how and when. The third stage is revision. BIM project documents are active – not only in the sense that they are in continual use throughout a project, but also in the way that they are adapted and developed. Project documents are updated in response to changes that take place during the project, particularly issues relating to information or the project management.

The documents that are used to manage the project carry as much legal weight as the contracts between the various parties grant them. In general, all BIM documents are considered to be contractual. Legal documentation is of course still required to ensure the status of BIM documentation as a legal requirement.

Employer's Information Requirements (EIR)

The EIR defines the information that must be produced during the project, forming a contractual requirement as one of the appendices of the BIM Protocol. The EIR may be created by the employer themselves or via an agent such as the project manager. It is a technical document that can be issued and updated before the commencement of each project stage; the content of the EIR is considered in detail in Chapter 8.

BIM Execution Plan (BEP)

The project team produces a BEP in response to the EIR to show how it will manage the creation, sharing and use of information on a project, including schedules, drawings and visual representations of designs. Each project BEP is unique, although they all have a common framework. A BEP should be created by a team effort, to ensure that the details it sets out are project- and team-specific. Every proposed team member identifies other team members whose responsibilities overlap with theirs, and indicates whether these overlaps are technical or spatial. For instance, if reinforced slopes or a sustainable drainage system are part of the scheme, the landscape architect and the civil engineer will need to liaise. The project team should align its activities with each of its members, ensuring that the appropriate human resources will be available at the agreed times to enable the project workflow to proceed as planned – a key difference in the way work is planned on a BIM project compared to traditional methods.

References

BSI (2007) *BS 1192:2007 Collaborative production of architectural, engineering and construction information. Code of practice.* London: British Standards Institution.

BSI (2013) *PAS 1192-2:2013 Specification for information management for the capital/delivery phase of assets using Building Information Modelling.* London: British Standards Institution.

BSI (2014a) *PAS 1192-3:2014 Specification for information management for the operational phase of assets using Building Information Modelling.* London: British Standards Institution.

BSI (2014b) *BS 1192-4:2014 Collaborative production of information Part 4: Fulfilling employers' information exchange requirements using COBie. Code of practice.* London: British Standards Institution.

BSI (2015) *PAS 1192-5:2015 Specification for security-minded building information modelling, digital built environments and smart asset management.* London: British Standards Institution.

CIC (2013) *Building Information Model (BIM) Protocol: Standard Protocol for use in projects using Building Information Models.* London: Construction Industry Council.

Government Soft Landings (2013) *Government Soft Landings micro-site.* London: Department for Business, Innovation and Skills. www.bimtaskgroup.org/gsl

NBS (2015a) *BIM Toolkit.* Newcastle upon Tyne: RIBA Enterprises. https://toolkit.thenbs.com

NBS (2015b) *Uniclass 2015.* Newcastle upon Tyne: RIBA Enterprises. https://toolkit.thenbs.com/articles/classification

CHAPTER 5

Collaborators

Introduction

BIM is intended to reduce costs and improve working practices while increasing quality and sustainability within the construction, management and redevelopment phases of a built asset's life cycle. Engineers, designers, contractors, facilities managers and employers all play a role in achieving these goals. This chapter introduces the team that makes a BIM project happen and looks at the nature of change that BIM implementation brings within a practice.

Collaboration is at the heart of BIM, resulting in more integrated design teams. The landscape practitioner has always connected the built and natural environment in professional terms, and does so in technical terms as well in BIM. When the entire project team is working from one 'source of truth' towards clearly defined and common goals, the result is higher collaborative capabilities, reduced risks in construction and improved built outcomes.

Project collaborators

Why try to find better ways to collaborate and coordinate information between consultants, suppliers and contractors? Because the ability to change the performance of an asset for the least cost occurs during the design phase, as illustrated in the MacLeamy curve (Figure 5.1). Furthermore, if one project team member is working in isolation without checking their work against that of others, the likely result is rework for someone either in the design phase or when the project is under construction and costs are higher. Sharing information across professions in the design stages can undoubtedly reduce the number of errors that go to site.

What does collaboration mean in a BIM environment? BIM Level 2 collaboration entails working to a project team BEP to which the whole team contributes (Figure 5.2). In a wider sense, a collaborative environment is one in which all project team members understand each other's work and responsibilities, and their relationship with the whole project. Roles and authorities are clear, and relationships are based on openness and cooperation. Clear collaboration processes enable several consultants to work on the same model simultaneously with identical information, so that changes by one consultant are visible in others' models. This section looks at the main partners in a collaborative BIM environment.

Figure 5.1 The MacLeamy curve presented a new way of thinking about cost

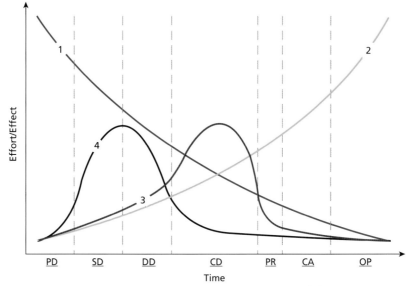

— 1 — Ability to impact cost and functional capabilities

— 2 — Cost of design changes

— 3 — Traditional design process

— 4 — Preferred design process

PD: Pre-design
SD: Schematic design
DD: Design development
CD: Construction documentation
PR: Procurement
CA: Construction Administration
OP: Operation

Employers

'Employer' is the generic term applied to a party procuring a BIM project, who will usually take ownership of the asset after handover. BIM Level 2 enables employers to shape the project brief and input to the project, using the EIR, the BIM Toolkit and GSL. The employer also manages collaboration between stakeholders within their own organisation and the project team; for instance, by ensuring that information released to them at data drops or information exchanges is passed to the agreed list of stakeholders.

The project team will want to consider the BIM maturity of an employer on a BIM project; employers should understand the prospective benefits of a BIM process, and have established how the information model of the completed asset will be used. An employer with a low BIM maturity may need to be guided in the preparation of an EIR and the requirements of GSL. A BIM project should serve the employer by reducing the lifetime cost of their landscape and assets, as well as providing a reliable development process. The team might look at whether the employer has an EIR, and if so who drafted it, who had input to it and what it is intended to achieve. They may also want to check whether the employer has specific performance indicators that must be met.

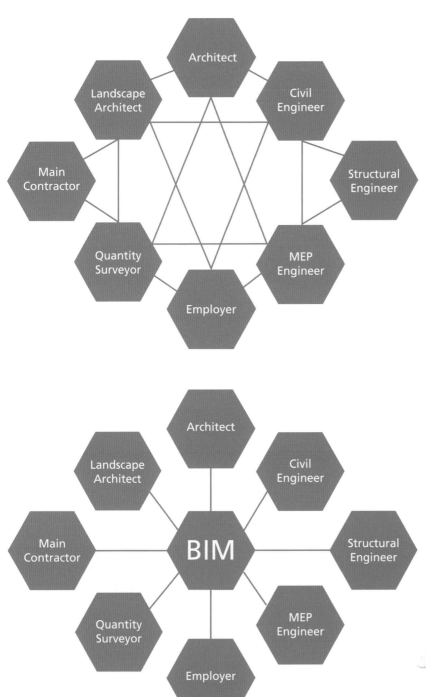

Figure 5.2
Communication on a BIM
project has a central point
of truth

Landscape and facilities managers

The employer should bring the facilities manager on board at the earliest opportunity, currently enabled by GSL and PAS 1192-2:2013 (BSI, 2013). Early involvement allows the facilities manager a say in how the project will be handed over to them at completion, and also provides a significant opportunity for them to engage with the allocation of costs and resources.

Designers, engineers and other consultants

There are many overlaps in areas of responsibility between the built environment industry's sectors. Interactions and interfaces between processes and technology should be agreed between these parties to ensure clear professional demarcations. No profession fully understands the practices of another, so reaching a mutual understanding of requirements and expectations helps facilitate the pursuit of a common goal. Designers and consultants will be more active at some stages than others, but the importance of ongoing communication with the other members of the project team remains, ensuring the development of a model that works for all.

Project managers

The project manager remains responsible for the allocation of responsibilities and programming in BIM, but has more tools available to implement the rigorous scheduling required. The role and responsibilities of each member of the project team are very clearly defined, so that the capacity of team members to meet the project programme is transparent. The BIM environment creates other new roles, discussed in the next chapter, with responsibilities for aspects of the management of projects, which are not necessarily the job of the project manager.

Main contractors

Main contractors are expected to have input early on in the life cycle of a BIM project, so that their knowledge of the coordination and management of construction and design can be incorporated from the start. BIM enables the main contractor to be well informed and to manage the logistics of a project much more effectively. The main contractor will take on the responsibilities of the lead designer and the project manager at the construction phase, if not earlier, with the project proceeding in the same vein. BIM Level 2 does not specify a contract structure such as design-build and is intended to work in any contractual or team structure context.

Specialist contractors

Specialist contractors, like main contractors, will be expected to give input to the design process in order to avoid physical or design rework once the project has gone to construction. Information provided by contractors is much more likely to be retained throughout the life cycle of the asset when it has a strong connection with the BIM model from the outset.

Suppliers

Suppliers can make information about their products available in a variety of digital formats for incorporation into a project team's BIM library. Product Data Templates (PDTs) supply detailed product information in a simple standardised format (see Chapter 15). Suppliers can provide quotes, estimates and specifications more readily earlier on in the project through the use of dynamic objects, which may be advantageous even if not specifically mandated by the EIR or BEP. Although specific supplier information is relevant primarily to the construction phase of a project, generic objects can be used in design and then replaced with manufacturer-specific objects. The earlier supply of information also benefits manufacturers, indicating the products that are needed and timescales.

Utilities

Obtaining utilities information can be a challenge. Services may be located on private land and not listed on a register, and utilities companies' records do not always show where an as-built service lies in the ground, with only indicative plans available. A site survey may therefore be the only way to establish what is on site and where. Although utilities providers could save significant costs to themselves and their customers by sharing information to avoid damage to underground services, there is currently no obligation to provide accurate digital plans to support the design and construction process. The capture and sharing of precise site information can be mandated by the EIR and the BEP survey strategy, discussed in Chapter 13. This reduces one of the principal risks of a built environment project – that of unforeseen ground conditions.

Statutory authorities

Statutory authorities will generally provide information on landscape designations and the assets that they manage in a computable form, usually GIS-based. Defra's MAGIC resource, holding geographic data on British rural, urban, coastal and marine environments, uses an interactive online map that shows information effectively, but is not directly available for download and use. Ordnance Survey data, although not all free of charge, are in a computable format that makes them a much more effective source for built environment projects.

Developing the project team

Practices can benefit from implementing BIM standards and processes in many ways. For instance, using a file-naming strategy that meets the BIM Level 2 standard is likely to improve information processes; training in software packages relevant to BIM will contribute to staff development, and so on. However, the greater benefits come when a BIM approach is adopted by an entire project team, and it is the project team that has the power to deliver these benefits.

Collaboration at its core meaning – working together – should be central to BIM implementation and is essential within a BIM project environment. Collaborationminded professionals are comfortable working with designers from other professions; they acknowledge that they cannot always solve problems alone, and will consult with others to work through difficulties. BIM processes are instigated and delivered by people, and in particular by people who collaborate.

There are various ways to procure the services of a design team for a construction project, many of which result in a staggered appointment whereby team members are brought in throughout the course of the project. It is therefore possible for new contractors or consultants to come on board after the BIM project documents have been agreed and the project is underway. One alternative is simultaneous appointment by the employer. BIM offers a major benefit to landscape practitioners in terms of involvement on a project from the outset, allowing the project team to decide working methodologies together from the start and enabling all the voices that should influence a design to be heard. This means that, for instance, from the earliest concept and outline phases the landscape architect can offer opinions on the arrangement of site objects that may be the principal responsibility of other consultants. It also means that information sharing for every stage can be planned jointly prior to commencement.

Lonely BIM and social BIM

It is possible to produce information models in isolation, without collaborating or sharing them with other members of project teams – a practice known as 'lonely BIM'. A practitioner may model an impressively complex object using software at the peak of its capability, but without the option to share information the usefulness of this modelling capacity is limited. Lonely BIM does not harness the full power of BIM. Engagement with stakeholders and partners reveals the information that they require, releasing the full benefits of a collaborative BIM environment for an employer and for a practitioner's own development.

In the early stages of BIM adoption, development processes are likely to take longer, so practices will want to see a suitable benefit from these changes. Changes can be characterised as upstream, parallel and downstream (Figure 5.3). An upstream change is where, for instance, a lead consultant integrates design efforts with their own to provide meaningful visualisations, clash assessment or other outputs. Parallel changes occur amongst stakeholders who are operating concurrently and use each other's input. Downstream changes affect stakeholders whose primary role

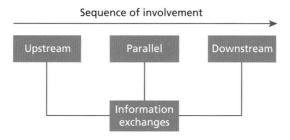

Figure 5.3 Upstream, downstream and parallel stakeholders

commences after the completion of the designers' work, such as facilities managers, maintenance and refurbishment contractors.

It is not always possible to foresee how design work or information produced during the design process will be used. Moreover, upstream, parallel and downstream stakeholders all require information to fulfil their own obligations. BIM's structured information management processes ensure that all pertinent information is available for project team members, delivered at the right level of maturity and in a format that others can use.

BIM does not require practitioners to work independently; it asks for collaboration in the sense of facilitating the work of others and being facilitated by others in return. This key concept requires one essential ingredient in BIM: digital information. Whether the employer wishes to take visualisations to public consultation, the drainage engineer needs a calculation of the amount of storm water run-off they need to manage, or the facilities manager wants to know the number of staff hours required to mow the site, BIM provides a more efficient means of achieving these outcomes that better meets the needs of stakeholders.

The change process

BIM is transforming the built environment sector in the short-to-medium term; it is not a quick fix for any of the industry's problems. Similarly at an organisational level it is not possible to become BIM-ready overnight. The BIM journey involves a process of gradual cultural change; it is not simply a matter of buying new software and implementing a new project document management system. BIM requires a review of a practice's systems and processes, but the subsequent change should be planned, managed and phased – not imposed at once, which can potentially cause disruption and put a practice at risk. Some questions to ask when changing information management processes are, for instance:

- Is full use being made of the information produced within a project?
- Is the information produced usable by all collaborators?
- Could more have been done to enhance the work of the project team?

It is helpful to have an understanding within the practice of the nature of change that BIM brings, so that staff know what is currently taking place, what will take place in the future, and what will not. This allows everyone to plan their work and to engage with the capabilities that the practice is developing. The change process that accompanies BIM does not mean that the roles of the designer or engineer become secondary, or that professional judgement is no longer required. What changes are the outputs, the process for delivering these outputs, and the ways that tools are used – the tools themselves may in fact remain the same. BIM is intended to streamline processes, and in doing so can allow designers to focus on design, by providing access to better information, enabling greater understanding of the consequences of design options earlier and freeing up time.

Reference

BSI (2013) *PAS 1192-2:2013 Specification for information management for the capital/delivery phase of assets using Building Information Modelling.* London: British Standards Institution.

CHAPTER 6

Roles

Introduction

This chapter introduces BIM-specific project roles, as distinct from the professional roles covered in the last chapter. BIM roles include an Information Manager, responsible for the preparation, storage and sharing of information, an Interface Manager, who works with the overlaps of consultants' design responsibilities, and a GSL Champion, coordinating delivery team outputs and client-side requirements. A BIM role is a set of tasks and responsibilities that may be assigned to one person or several people; it does not necessarily correspond to a specific individual. It is also possible for one person to have a number of BIM roles, so that, for instance, a landscape architect could take the role of Information Manager in addition to their professional design input. These roles are assigned by the employer, but may equally well be allocated by a project team. This chapter briefly introduces the new roles; the responsibilities that accompany each are detailed in Chapter 12.

Background

Much more recorded interaction takes place between consultants in a BIM Level 2 project, facilitated by the Information Manager and Interface Manager. A project team or the employer nominates the overall project's Information Manager (Figure 6.1). Each task team (the sub-teams responsible for delivery of specific aspects of the project) has a Task Team Information Manager and a Task Team Interface Manager; again these roles could be undertaken by the same person. Their duties are not entirely new and have been performed on a largely ad hoc basis hitherto, but in BIM are clearly defined to provide a firm foundation for collaboration and information management. These roles create a greater level of transparency within a project team, which benefits all parties. A better awareness of the work that is being carried out within the team can make for the smoother operation of a project, with lower overheads and less rework.

In addition, the roles of BIM Coordinator and BIM Manager have been adopted by industry, although they have no official definition as they are not covered by the BIM Level 2 standards. As bespoke roles, their specific responsibilities vary from practice to practice, but they generally relate to information management and the implementation of BIM standards.

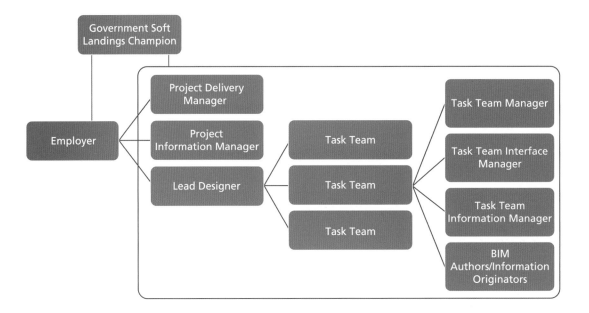

Figure 6.1 How the BIM
Level 2 roles relate to one
another

Information Manager

The project team Information Manager maintains the CDE, and determines how project files are named and stored. The Information Manager may not have any design input, but does have ultimate responsibility for the format in which files are saved and their handling prior to sharing with the project team. They deal with interoperability issues and make sure that the project team plans its information exchanges accordingly. This level of control ensures that the information and files shared by project team members meet the employer's requirements and are usable by those who need them.

Interface Manager

Each task team appoints an Interface Manager who works with the professional and technical interfaces between consultants, encouraging collaboration between task teams and beneficial interactions between designs. This could include, for instance, identifying where objects created by members of one profession could affect those designed by another. A natural play area incorporating a sustainable drainage system would involve both a spatial and a technical interface; in a BIM project, the Interface Manager would be responsible for ensuring that both elements functioned effectively.

Government Soft Landings Champion

The GSL Champion is a third-party facilitator who liaises with all parties throughout the project to see that the ongoing work reflects the employer's and users' requirements and that the team is preparing for handover from the outset.

Other roles

Other roles are included within the BIM Level 2 standards, as shown in Figure 6.1. The Task Team Manager has responsibility for authorising the issue of work, BIM Authors generate the models, and the employer's representative and technical adviser represent the employer's organisation. They may also be responsible for generating the vision and managing the value consideration for the project. The design lead and contractor lead are considered to be the Tier 1 leads of a project.

The importance of information management

Information management facilitates connected information – which means more usable information. A standardised Product Data Sheet, for instance, provides the landscape architect with specification data for designs, the logistics manager with information to calculate transport costs, and the quantity surveyor with the ability to compare products and ensure that the project operates within cost parameters.

Rational, accountable decisions require robust information. BIM creates connections between decision-making processes throughout the life cycle of a project, structures for meeting the employer's specific requirements, and metrics against which the project can be assessed. Standardisation within a BIM environment means that changes are more closely controlled, so that information received by the employer and members of the project team provides a more stable platform for decision-making. This minimises the late changes to design that can reduce quality, create uncertainty and increase costs.

Shared standardised information also benefits sustainability objectives, allowing calculations regarding carbon savings and recycling, as well as waste reduction. All this is possible without standardised files, but in a BIM project this information can be used at the design stage for maximum benefit.

CHAPTER 7

The BIM Implementation Plan

Introduction

Implementing BIM within a practice – and on a project – requires planning. Having considered the organisational implications and prerequisites, the people and technology involved, and the standards that govern the process, this chapter now looks at creating a BIM Implementation Plan: the final step to becoming ready to work on live BIM Level 2 projects.

The Implementation Plan manages the process of implementing BIM within a practice, and is the key planning tool for the entire BIM journey. As a working document, it requires regular review as the practice responds to changes, both within the team and in the external environment. More than this, it sets out what BIM means to a practice; it aligns with the practice's aspirations and business plan and sets out a clear focus for the future. For now, this chapter outlines the contents of an implementation plan, and looks at the factors that shape it.

Approaches to BIM implementation

A four-stage implementation process is suggested. The first step is to make the business case or set out the rationale for change, defining the strategic outcomes that the practice seeks to achieve. The next stage is to assess current processes and structures and the extent to which they align with the business case. Having gained an understanding of where the practice wants to be and a clear picture of how existing ways of working relate to these aims, the practice can generate a strategy to enable it to achieve its objectives. Once implemented, these changes can be reviewed against the initial business case to assess whether the desired outcomes have been realised. This may be a cyclical process or a linear progression. In either case, the aim is to understand the reasons for implementing BIM, the nature of the changes involved and the best way to carry them out.

A cyclical, iterative process of BIM implementation (Figure 7.1) moves rapidly through the project stages several times. This allows early progress to be made, quickly highlighting problems before moving on to the next phase. The cyclical method is best applied to areas of BIM implementation with less certain outcomes, when it not known exactly what the end result should be. Alternatively, the linear or waterfall approach (shown in Figure 7.2) works through the same stages but

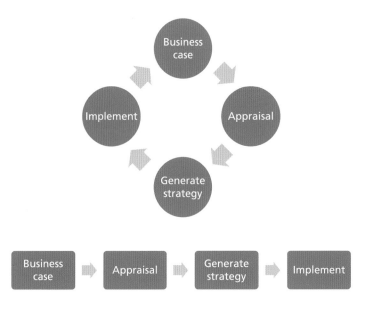

Figure 7.1
Implementation cycle

Figure 7.2
Implementation flow

thoroughly and once only. It gives the project well-defined objectives, and is best used when those objectives are clearly understood, as there is less scope for returning to decisions once made.

In reality the process of BIM implementation is rarely either entirely sequential or cyclical. It is unlikely that planning, testing and doing will proceed in a simple and straightforward manner; it is more likely that some processes will be introduced simultaneously, and smaller sub-projects implementing different aspects of BIM will emerge.

The four stages of making the business case, appraisal, generating strategy and finally implementation are covered in the rest of this chapter.

Business case

Decision-makers will be able to grasp the strategic implications of BIM implementation by considering the types of changes that BIM can bring to a practice, which might include, for instance, changes in technology, process, business and team capability. An analysis of these changes might include asking questions such as:

• What are the drivers? Greater efficiency? Winning more work?
• What is the extent of anticipated change – large or small scale? Would it affect parts of the practice in different ways?
• Who would be affected? Will people's roles change?
• What policies will need to be in place?
• What processes will need to change?
• Where does the practice want to be? What differences in thinking and understanding would be required? And is the practice ready?

The business case for BIM implementation is the justification for undertaking change, and provides the ultimate test for the continuation of the BIM implementation project. As a management tool, it also creates a consistency of approach in delivering implementation.

Vision

The BIM vision is the overriding theme that develops BIM implementation. It should link with the practice's existing strategy and vision so that BIM implementation represents a continuation of current strategic planning. The vision orientates a practice at every level and demonstrates to clients the direction in which the practice is moving. The BIM vision should be carefully worded in plain language to be easily understood by all.

The benefits that a practice seeks to gain from BIM implementation should align with its vision, and it is against these benefits that the value of implementation is measured. Different types of benefits derive from BIM implementation depending on how the practice operates. These can be characterised as:

- *Diversification*: offering more services
- *Efficiency*: offering the same services at reduced rates
- *Enhancement*: offering services that rival or exceed competitors'

Benefits may fall into more than one category, and should be quantifiable to ensure that progress can be monitored.

Costs

Financial implications must be managed effectively throughout the period of BIM implementation. Costs arise mainly from the time required to manage and implement processes, plus any training and software costs. Cost planning should be in place to measure progress against the costs incurred.

Timescale

Managing the timescale for the process of BIM implementation involves developing a programme, setting milestones and regular review. Tools such as Gantt charts can be used to help formulate a logical and clearly manageable sequence of events. Frequent review cycles are usually the most appropriate, depending on resources available. Many innovation processes operate cyclically, however, and it can be harder to define a beginning and end to this type of process, especially if the outcomes are not fully known. An ongoing review of progress against the business case should enable effective monitoring and allow informed decisions to be made on the implementation process as it moves forward.

Performance indicators

A business case should include key performance indicators (KPIs), relevant to the practice's own strategy, culture and capabilities. Research by organisations such as BRE and Constructing Excellence may be of use in deciding relevant indicators.

Risks and opportunities

Risk management is an essential part of ensuring the success of BIM implementation, as in any innovation strategy. Managing risk does not have to be about damage limitation and reduction only; it can also present opportunities and benefits for the employer and the practice. Also when a risk is averted or ameliorated, the costs avoided can be considered a benefit. Types of risk, and accompanying opportunities, can be categorised as:

- *Strategic* – affecting overall business strategy
  A strategic risk might be, for example, making a flawed business case for BIM, or not delivering the required changes during the BIM implementation process. A strategic opportunity could be the chance to expand into a new market or offer new services.
- *Operational* – occurring in the supply of a product
  Rising design or staffing costs, or loss of information on a project present operational risks; the discovery of new workflows that reduce costs is an operational opportunity. Operational risk is inherently linked to financial risk, as the liability for the costs of operating remain within the practice until payment is received.
- *Financial* – including all risks associated with the operation of a practice and the built environment industry as a whole
  Costly operating methods or outlays that contribute to a poor return on investment are financial risks. Developing services that improve revenue possibilities or reduce overheads is a financial opportunity.
- *Compliance* – associated with a project's legal requirements
  Failure to adhere to the standards and regulations required on a project is a compliance risk; implementing the project and UK BIM standards reduces the likelihood of unforeseen and unpaid amendments to the project, and provides greater financial security to the practice as a result.
- *External* – outside a practice's control
  A software supplier going out of business is an external risk; new software that can improve the quality of work is an opportunity.

BIM-specific risks

A number of concerns specific to BIM implementation are sometimes raised:

- *Competitive bids*
  The bidding process operates differently in a BIM Level 2 environment and requires additional prequalification material, so practices may experience some initial uncertainty in meeting the new criteria.
- *Market readiness*
  There have been suggestions that the built environment sector is not yet able to supply the demand for BIM. However, there is now a wealth of highly developed BIM practice, and the landscape profession is increasingly ready to supply and make use of BIM, as are other professions. There could still be the risk that

business processes or software use are not at the stage of readiness required to achieve a specific project's goals, of course.

- *Contracts*
  The correct legal and BIM documentation must be included in a contract, ensuring that BIM processes are a legal obligation within the project. The contract retains priority over BIM unless a specific addendum regarding the legal position of BIM is included. The BIM Protocol (CIC, 2013) should be included with contracts, its two appendices defining the employer's requirements in terms of the content and timing of information delivery.
- *Model ownership*
  Model ownership is covered by the BIM Protocol, and assures legal rights over intellectual property as agreed in the contract with the employer.
- *Legal issues*
  The BIM Level 2 standards have so far remained largely untested in case law, but legal challenges could still potentially change the requirements for implementation. Concerns have been raised regarding liability for models, despite the relative comfort that many within the legal profession who have taken an interest in BIM have expressed. Professional advice should be sought on specific aspects of implementation as required.

Appraisal

The business case for BIM can be assessed against existing project processes. Identifying the risks and opportunities outlined above as they relate to human resources and IT infrastructure will also help clarify the practice's existing BIM capabilities. The appraisal process aims to create an understanding of the organisational context and culture, and identify opportunities for integrating BIM workflows. Appraisal cycles will consider how the strategy and subsequent implementation have and will affect a practice's existing processes. Practices find their own balance between standardisation and innovation, weighing the need for responsiveness and flexibility against the need for consistency.

Qualitative or quantitative appraisals of existing tasks can be carried out, including their strengths and weaknesses. If BIM implementation is undertaken to improve workflows, for example, devising criteria to compare how tasks are completed within the old and new systems can enable a like-for-like comparison. More sophisticated approaches could include process mapping using business process or function modelling methodologies such as IDEF0 (Integrated Definition for Function Modelling), project management techniques such as Prince 2 or Agile techniques such as SCRUM. Once an approach has been decided, existing processes can be examined to understand current collaborative processes, and how workloads are managed, tasks carried out and deliverables produced.

Standardisation and innovation

This element of the appraisal could begin by examining how a practice's existing standards relate to BIM implementation; for example, in allocating human resources to projects, or software use. An analysis of how change already takes place within the practice will be helpful, and is likely to highlight members of staff who are key to driving and enabling change.

Process and technology

BIM is said to be a process enabled by technology, but the relationship between process and technology is a complex one. Mapping the existing hardware and software in use within the practice can show what its capabilities are and where opportunities for development lie. Areas where process changes will occur should be identified, as they could affect how bidding and projects are managed.

Insurance

A well-managed BIM process will often be perceived to reduce risk to a practice. Insurers will be able to advise on the insurance issues associated with implementing new processes. When discussing BIM with regard to professional indemnity insurance, it is important to consider the information management and BIM-specific roles and responsibilities to be undertaken. Any relevant documentation including the BIM Implementation Plan and BEP should be available for the insurer to view. Issues that may affect a practice's insurance policy include:

- liability exclusions on loss of digital documents or models
- any particular storage or backup requirements for digital information
- whether the practice is hosting the CDE
- whether the practice is undertaking the role of information management
- the BIM Protocols that are to be used
- the required Level of Detail at each stage
- data exchange and the measures for accountability and auditing
- limitations of liability on automated model checking software

The Landscape Institute's Technical Advice Note on PI insurance (Landscape Institute, 2013) gives further guidance.

Generate strategy

Getting work

Bidding for a BIM project means dealing with additional questions at the PQQs stage. PAS 91 (BSI, 2013) is the standard prequalification questionnaire for the built environment sector and contains guidance that will be used by those creating prequalification questionnaires. Standardised assessment documents provide the opportunity to demonstrate general capability, but a more in-depth assessment between members of the prospective project team is necessary to ensure that the task teams would be able to share information effectively.

Some documents that are required as part of a BIM project bid assess a practice's BIM and IT capabilities, so this will need to be factored into future bidding processes.

Generic BIM assessment forms are available on the Construction Project Information Committee website (www.cpic.org.uk/cpix). If they are used in generating the business case and appraising existing capabilities, they can also help inform the goals of the implementation strategy.

Project management

There are a number of new roles in BIM Level 2 as outlined in the previous chapter. Consultants will be required to work within these new capacities and new approaches to managing deliverables, in order to avoid operational and financial risks.

Process

Many operations will be standardised by BIM Level 2. This does not spell the end of design innovation and invention, but does mean some planning. The nature of information flows between team members and within a project team affects the quality of the information produced. Are these workflows highly structured or ad hoc? If information goes through rework, how is this managed? The BIM Toolkit will define the deliverables required at every stage, and the Level of Detail.

Project documentation

The BIM Level 2 process is a highly documented one. The approach to managing this information should consider not only the BIM documents that will be used, but also how they will be created, updated and reviewed.

Software

The landscape practitioner requires design, coordination, specification and costing software tools to produce the information required for a BIM project, and will need greater levels of embedded information. It will be helpful to map the information that is to be input, the actions that can be performed on those inputs and the outputs required. This process will show how geometry and information are transferred from one software package to another. The standards for file naming and layer or object naming will need to align with BIM Level 2 standards. Other processes to ensure that digital information is reusable and editable will need to be taken into account. A web browser is often required to access software services, and will usually need to be kept up to date for security reasons. A change of browser will be needed if the one currently in use is not supported by the software.

Many BIM solutions from the major software providers target sectors significantly larger than landscape, so their landscape provision may not meet requirements. One option is to work with smaller software developers, either to adapt existing software, or to explore new packages with solutions more suited to landscape practice. A practice's existing operating system will determine which software packages can be used; however, the primary consideration should be finding the software packages that will produce the deliverables required and meet the practice's needs.

Hardware

BIM Level 2 relies on remote storage of files on the CDE, defined in BS 1192:2007 (BSI, 2007), which requires suitable local area networks and internet connections. Software specifications will need to be checked to ensure compatibility with existing hardware and networks; the supplier's website or a representative can provide this information.

IT Security

Protocols for sharing and storing information will require review, as data security and integrity are primary concerns in a BIM environment. The practice should determine its IT security requirements independently of the BIM implementation process, as a general rule. There are, however, IT security considerations associated with a BIM environment, and a security strategy should also incorporate the employer's security protocols where relevant. Highly sensitive projects will require higher levels of security. PAS 1192-5 (BSI, 2015) applies to security-minded projects and requires specific information management practices; the practice will also need to comply with the built asset's information security requirements.

User policy

A user policy ensures that security and access are correctly managed within the practice and project team. A hierarchy of users is the preferred methodology for managing IT security; most users, including managers, have restricted capabilities to install software.

Standardisation

Some practice standards will need to be updated to encompass the changes brought by BIM. These should be integrated into existing office management documents and reviewed regularly as BIM implementation develops.

Innovation

Much academic research has already been done on BIM, including its landscape applications, which can inform an innovation strategy. Other sources that may be useful are buildingSMART guides, the BIMTalk website, and the BIM section of the Landscape Institute's website.

Training

New standards for the use of software and other changes in processes and operations required by BIM Level 2 will require staff training.

Implementation strategy

Implementing BIM does not happen as a one-off; it involves iterations over time to build upon the lessons learnt. As milestones and targets are set, options for beginning to apply BIM on projects can be considered.

Dry run

Before going live with BIM processes and technology, it is wise to test out capabilities internally and with partners. Checking information connections between project team members helps avoid future costs of poor coordination. This could include simple essential software operations such as sharing files with new naming strategies and checking they work as expected, and ensuring that models are correctly located and that information transfers in a usable format.

Competitions

There are a number of free-to-enter competitions such as Build Live events and BIMStorm that provide an opportunity to practise collaborative aspects of BIM with other teams, in a condensed project from start to finish.

Test projects

Test projects can offer considerable clarity, from checking software to cooperation with other consultants, and can take much of the guesswork out of the implementation process. The opportunity to focus on particular aspects of a project can help progress specific areas of implementation.

Live projects

It is, however, possible to implement BIM gradually on live projects. This allows the cost of BIM implementation to be partially covered by fees, and the lessons learnt will be directly applicable to future projects. However, it is harder to assess the consequences of implementation, so the team will need to make extra time for the process of reviewing progress, learning and adaptation. A fall-back option should be in place in case the practice turns out not to be quite BIM-ready.

Training strategy

People are the most important resource in BIM implementation and developing their capacity is key. Assessing individuals' existing skills and training needs is important, from knowledge of BIM processes to software competence, but a general policy for each tier of the practice will help ensure essential BIM capabilities; managers will need to be able to review BIM outputs, for instance.

A skills register can be used to record team members' BIM capabilities and expectations for developing their skills in future. Some staff will be keen to develop, and others may need to be reminded of the benefits of professional and personal development. Either way, investing time and money in training pays dividends; the practice will be better able to achieve its goals, and will see gains from using existing resources more effectively, increasing staff retention and attracting higher calibre candidates.

Training should be relevant to landscape. Whether provided by a landscape professional or by a landscape-focused organisation, sector-specific training offers significant benefits. Training can be self-led learning, internal training sessions or formal external courses, as determined by the practice's resources. From a cold start, it is wise to employ a trainer to give an overview of the software and interactive sessions. This also applies to BIM Level 2 processes; any training should relate specifically to projects or take place on a test project. Training sessions or training on projects can be a good way to improve competencies beyond the core BIM staff. Self-led training is also vital, in particular reading the BIM Level 2 documents and testing software and new ideas.

References

BSI (2007) *BS 1192:2007 Collaborative production of architectural, engineering and construction information. Code of practice.* London: British Standards Institution.

BSI (2013) *PAS 91:2013 Construction prequalification questionnaires.* London: British Standards Institution.

BSI (2015) *PAS 1192-5:2015 Specification for security-minded building information modelling, digital built environments and smart asset management.* London: British Standards Institution.

CIC (2013) *Building Information Model (BIM) Protocol: Standard Protocol for use in projects using Building Information Models.* London: Construction Industry Council.

Landscape Institute (2013) *Implications of Building Information Modelling (BIM) on Professional Indemnity (PI) Insurance* (Technical Advice Note 01/13). London: Landscape Institute.

PART II

IMPLEMENTATION

Introduction

BIM represents a sea-change in the construction industry. For instance, BIM Level 2:

- shares design information collaboratively
- engages every project stakeholder
- creates a single point of truth for all project information
- gives project teams new roles and responsibilities
- manages information and programmes with rigour and clarity

Preparations for BIM-readiness were covered in Part I; Part II deals with running a BIM Level 2 project, from tendering through to handover, and beyond. The benefits of BIM can be seen as early as the pre-contract phase, in terms of gaining an understanding of the employer's needs and those of future collaborators and project team members. Once a contract is awarded, information management and collaboration processes within the team develop, and BIM workflows come into play. Moving through the design and development phase, Part II ends with handover and the asset in use. A BIM project starts with the end-user in mind, and the engagement of landscape managers and users is a significant benefit of BIM in landscape, enabling effective management and maintenance, and the design of landscapes that are fit for purpose.

With this is mind, Part II explores in more depth the specific issues in running a BIM Level 2 project, following both the letter and the spirit of the guidance, such as:

- responding to the employer's requirements at tender stage with a BIM Execution Plan (BEP)
- working with or in the new roles and relationships involved in a BIM project
- using the key project tools
- creating information management systems
- engaging with managers of the landscape and facilities and its end-users

Although many BIM Level 2 processes are standardised, there are always aspects of individual BIM projects that are unique. Factors such as the employer's and the project team's BIM maturity will play a part in how BIM is realised on the project. There are many decisions that must be taken on a BIM Level 2 project, which although also necessary in non-BIM projects, may not be explicitly specified. The majority of these questions relate to collaborative working and information exchange. These processes together lead to the design of a coordinated, well-defined, constructible project with few or no defects – the most frequently cited benefit of BIM.

CHAPTER 8

Employer's Information Requirements

Introduction

An employer issues an EIR as part of a brief and tender documentation. It sets out the project's information requirements, and asks bidders to respond with a BIM Execution Plan (BEP) demonstrating their capacity to complete the works. After its initial issue, the EIR is refined and developed and finally becomes part of the contract, at which point the project team is obliged to deliver its requirements throughout the project life cycle.

This chapter looks first at the purpose of the EIR, then covers its specific technical, management and commercial requirements. As this chapter is intended to be of use to practitioners submitting a response to an EIR as well as those creating them in the capacity of employer's representative, it explains some of the thinking behind the EIR's different sections to help employers and bidders make best use of this document.

Purpose of the EIR

An employer uses an EIR to inform consultants tendering for work how information is used in their organisation, and their requirements for information delivery and management. The initial EIR is a starting point for discussion of the project plan, and allows bidding teams to bring their own professional judgement and input to the brief. Bidders may raise queries about the EIR before submitting a final response, and any changes made by the employer must be issued to all prospective project teams. The EIR can therefore undergo revision, with new versions issued as requirements are defined and the project brief develops.

The EIR is eventually written into the project contracts as one of the appendices of the BIM Protocol (CIC, 2013). It can be considered finalised once it specifies all the information requirements that must be included in contracts with the project team. The employer should be aware that in order for the EIR to become a contractual requirement, the BIM Protocol must be included within the contract documents with the EIR in the information requirements appendix.

Requirements of the EIR

The EIR should frame the questions that the employer wants BEPs to answer. The employer's requirements should be SMART – specific, measurable, achievable, realistic and time-bound – and should follow the essence of lean practice, saying no more than needs to be said to get the job done, and avoiding duplication of responsibilities. Strict parameters for information management should be included only where specifically required; if an employer requests the provision of information with which they are unfamiliar, they should rely on bidders to propose how this information could be managed. Sections may be left blank where the employer has no preference, or wants to let the appointed project team respond. The EIR should not preclude innovation, or deter bidders from providing value.

A project team should be satisfied that the EIR can meet the needs of the project. It is essential that the EIR relates specifically to the planned project and the requirements of its users and the employer; arbitrary requirements can negate the BIM ethos of low waste and high innovation. As a technical document, it should normally be created with input from the design or construction lead or similar within the prospective project team. It should be drafted with due regard to the integrated design team, to avoid focus on any one professional specialism or aspect of the project.

An EIR should include any unresolved decisions, along with their potential effects. The employer may be considering phasing in new software with implications for the management of assets, for instance. The EIR should note this, as the project team will need to ensure that the Asset Information Model (AIM) they produce to maintain and manage the asset post-handover is compatible with the new system. Planning for 'known unknowns' enables the project team to respond in the BEP and reduce risks of time or cost over-run. The BEP and EIR create a dialogue, establishing ways to make the information management and collaborative working aspects of the project achievable.

While roles are not specifically allocated at the outset, it is advisable for the prospective project team to nominate an Information Manager and a Project Delivery Manager, responsible for delivering the project, at the earliest opportunity. The relationship between these roles and the bidding team helps define how information management and collaborative working develop on the project.

As with any project brief, an employer's capacity to produce an effective EIR depends on their experience, knowledge and quality of advice. A frequently procuring client such as a university, government body, supermarket or other asset-rich organisation will be able to create detailed EIR documents, having large amounts of information and lessons learnt from previous construction projects on which to draw. Conversely, a client procuring a built asset for the first time is likely to create a less detailed EIR and project brief. The BIM Task Group offers guidance and sample content in a model EIR that employers may use (www.bimtaskgroup.org/bim-eirs). The EIR's standard contents are set out by the BIM Task Group under the headings Technical, Management and Commercial, which are discussed in the following sections of this chapter (Figure 8.1).

Technical	Management	Commercial
• Software platforms • Data exchange format • Coordinates • Level of Detail • Training	• Standards • Roles and responsibilities • Planning the work and data segregation • Security • Coordination and clash detection process • Collaboration process • Model review meetings • Health and safety and Construction Design Management • Systems performance • Compliance plan • Delivery strategy for asset information	• Data drops and project deliverables • Client's strategic purposes • Defined BIM/Project deliverables • BIM-specific competence assessment • File types

Technical

The technical information section is where the employer details their IT and data infrastructure, with which bidders will be required to work.

Figure 8.1 Contents of an EIR

Software platforms

This section identifies the employer's software platforms. Any built environment project involves a wide range of software, from accounting, project management, facilities management and time sheet packages to GIS, modelling and specification systems. The employer may prescribe software if the AIM will need to integrate with their existing or planned systems; this is not the place for consultants to include their own software preferences. The EIR should state the requirements of the employer's internal systems, such as any electronic document management systems (EDMSs), which may have their own naming conventions.

Data exchange format

The employer should specify data exchange formats to facilitate information exchange with their team, creating a useful body of asset information for management and maintenance post-handover. Centrally procured projects will require COBie format information, the standardised information exchange protocol; other file formats may include specific data exchange formats such as IFC (Industry Foundation Classes).

Coordinates

The EIR defines spatial coordination arrangements. Coordinates should always extend to the site boundary and include a recognised geographic coordinate system (GCS), representing the position and context of the project with an appropriate origin specific to the site, expressed in the format of the GCS in use. This point must be located accurately as it is the foundation for the coordination of the project throughout the asset's life cycle. Interoperability issues can occur in the area of spatial coordination, particularly when moving between the building envelope and the landscape. Units should be defined where appropriate to the needs of the project, in conjunction with the correct positioning of the site origin. Scale may be unified across disciplines or each discipline may be required to define their units in the BEP. For further information see BS 1192:2007 Project Space Statement (BSI, 2007: 26).

Level of Detail: general and component

This is a complex area. Employers with sufficient experience or expertise within their team will be able to complete this section, but should otherwise seek advice from the project team or a third party. The Level of Detail or LoD will be defined by an agreement between the project team and the employer within the post-contract BEP, and can then be written into the BIM Protocol appendices to form a contractual requirement.

The EIR will define general and component Levels of Detail for the project. The general Level of Detail refers to the level of development of a model. This means that a model delivered at a given project stage should be suitable for that stage; a general LoD would require that at concept stage, models can be relied upon for their conceptual contents, for example. Component Level of Detail refers to the levels of graphical detail and information required for specific components. For instance, if a local authority requires that its own bespoke bollards are used on projects within its boundary, the level of component detail will be higher than the general model. The BIM Toolkit can be used to inform the LoD required for the project and components at each stage.

An important factor to be considered within the EIR is the format in which the LoD should be presented. There are a number of LoD standards, which are covered in Chapter 19. The EIR's Level of Detail section informs the Model Production and Delivery Table (MPDT), showing the models that are to be produced and the LoD for each data drop, or information exchange (Figure 8.2).

Figure 8.2 An example Model Production and Delivery Table using PAS 1192-2:2013. This shows a default nominal Level of Detail required, which relates directly to the EIR. Data drops are information handovers that inform the employer's decision-making points at project milestones.

	Drop 1 Stage 1		Drop 2a Stage 2		Drop 2b Stage 2		Drop 3 Stage 3		Drop 4 Stage 6	
	Model originator	Level of Detail	Model originator	Level of Detail	Model originator	Level of Detail	Model originator	Level of Detail	Model originator	Level of Detail
Overall form and content										
Space planning	Landscape Architect	1	Landscape Architect	2	Landscape Contractor	2	Landscape Contractor	3	Landscape Contractor	6
Site and context	Landscape Architect	1	Landscape Architect	2	Landscape Contractor	2	Landscape Contractor	3	Landscape Contractor	6
Sustainable drainage system	Civil Engineer	1	Civil Engineer	2	Landscape Contractor	2	Landscape Contractor	3	Landscape Contractor	6
Construction phasing	Landscape Architect	1	Landscape Architect	2	Landscape Contractor	2	Landscape Contractor	3	Landscape Contractor	6
Health and safety design	Landscape Architect	1	Landscape Architect	2	Landscape Contractor	2	Landscape Contractor	3	Landscape Contractor	6

Training

This section specifies any training necessary to meet the employer's requirements and ensure that project outputs are up to standard. A key feature of BIM Level 2 is collaborative working with aligned project deliverables and milestones, and training on these essential requirements may be needed. Training may also be required to enable relevant staff to pass information and models from the construction phase on to the employer and asset and facility management team effectively. Training should be stipulated only where there are specific requirements for the project, and the employer should make these explicit at the time of tender.

Management

This section forms the most substantial part of the EIR, setting out the management processes to be adopted on the project.

Standards

The EIR should include details of the standards documents to be used on the project, which at BIM Level 2 will include:

- PAS 1192-2:2013 (BSI, 2013)
- PAS:1192-3:2014 (BSI, 2014a)
- BS 1192-4:2014 (BSI, 2014b)
- GSL (Government Soft Landings, 2013)
- Uniclass and the NBS BIM Toolkit (NBS, 2015a and 2015b).

Others include recognised standards defining the employer's management systems or data protection; other information management or collaboration standards may be included.

Roles and responsibilities

The specific roles defined in PAS 1192-2:2013 will be assigned here. This section should cover the need for information and interface management at a project-wide level as well as within each team; there may also be scope to include further roles dependent upon the project. BIM roles were introduced in Chapter 5 and their responsibilities are detailed in Chapter 12.

Planning the work and data segregation

This section shows how the modelling process will be managed. The processes of planning the work and data segregation are usually prescribed by the employer and the lead designer in the first instance, but the details will require negotiation to specify the exact information to be produced. The planning of work should be included within the EIR in order to give activities the status of contractual obligation.

Data segregation defines how information handover and distinction between specific pieces of work will be maintained. The project team can confirm their compliance with this requirement by undertaking to adhere to the CDE usage standards. If a specialist sub-contractor's information is fed into their direct employer's submission, it should be specified at which points this handover will occur.

The naming convention for the project is defined in this section. Model management covers how and where the model is stored. Access privileges and timings of access should be given particular consideration by the employer if information is sensitive. This aspect of the EIR will be developed more as the project brief and EIR develop. When the EIR becomes a contractual document, responsibilities for models should be defined in a MPDT.

Security

This section of the EIR should refer to PAS 1192-5 (BSI, 2015); requirements will depend on the sensitivity of the project. The employer's IT managers will specify requirements for compliance with their security standards, which should be entered here. If normal levels of security are involved, general good practice for working securely in an online environment will suffice, such as using strong passwords and preventing unauthorised access to computers or files. More sensitive project information will require higher levels of security, however. UK government projects will need to have additional processes and policies in place for reporting, managing and resolving security incidents, and staff training to ensure an appropriate understanding of security.

Coordination and clash detection process

Clash detection uses spatial coordination in the design stages to identify where disruptive, dangerous or costly mistakes could occur. These are then resolved in the virtual model before construction commences, avoiding waste, expense and delays. Bidders should state the process for coordinating and checking models produced by task teams, and whether a specific file format or software package will be used for clash avoidance purposes.

Collaboration process

This section asks bidders to demonstrate their understanding of and competencies in the cultural requirements for working as a team towards a common goal. Team-building exercises and workshopping ideas can foster a collaborative ethos, as can regularly meeting together as a project group from the outset. Other more formal means could include procurement tools such as partnering, and different contract systems.

Model review meetings

The process for joint deliberation of model development is set out in this section. The employer, with input from the appointed project team, will expand their initial intentions into a workable and cost-effective process for model review. The timings, process and attendees will be defined in the EIR as part of the contract, but may begin with more general requirements. A statutory authority may request workshops and public consultation, for example, so a cycle of meetings at a given frequency with specific purposes will be needed, along with spatial coordination, clash detection, cost management and other project needs.

Health and safety and Construction Design Management (CDM)

This section of the EIR sets out the employer's and the project team's compliance requirements. The EIR should describe any information management policies supporting the project's health and safety and CDM requirements. The key obligations under UK legislation, according to the Health and Safety Executive, are improvement of the planning and management of projects from the very start, identification of risks early on, targeted effort where it can do the most good in terms of health and safety, and the reduction of unnecessary bureaucracy.

The Construction (Design and Management) Regulations 2015 make the principal designer or lead designer responsible for managing much of the health and safety aspects of a project. This person should therefore coordinate an information requirements and information management strategy to fulfil their obligations. Other members of the project team also need information to be able to fulfil their own duties, so an information exchange mechanism should be agreed as part of the BIM planning process.

More generally, BIM Level 2 processes do much to meet the management of health and safety requirements. For example, those responsible for managing site risks can receive higher quality information earlier in the project life cycle, with 3D and specification information available to improve the management of site activities. Staff can be trained in potential risks on site using a 3D model walkthrough, and any hazardous materials and objects can be easily identified within the model, so that appropriate handling and management processes can be put in place.

Systems performance

A BIM Level 2 project will normally see an AIM produced to assist the employer in managing the facility after handover. To this end, this section of the EIR sets out the strengths and weaknesses of the employer's systems, in terms of working with project information outputs or software constraints that may present interoperability issues, for instance. The employer's IT managers will probably need to be consulted about the organisation's capabilities, security policies, available software, ability to process files of varying complexity and size, and maintenance plans.

Compliance plan

The compliance plan asks how models and other data will be coordinated and maintained. This means definition of the system storing models, either as offered by the bid team or the employer's preferred option. The compliance requirements will draw on the standards section of the EIR and are negotiated during the pre-contract BEP.

The EIR may require the bidder to supply assurances regarding the accuracy of their models or their selection of products, and their incorporation of that information into the model. Any specific quality assurance (QA) mechanisms used by the employer will be detailed here, particularly where they are embedded within their process and software systems. If unstated, an industry-wide QA standard, such as ISO 9001, may be used. A compliance plan for a UK government construction project from 2016 will require the bidder to describe how they intend to meet their duties to the end-user under the requirements of GSL (Government Soft Landings).

Delivery strategy for asset information

This section of the EIR requires bidders to outline their approach to keeping the employer's systems up to date with relevant information throughout the project's key stages and data drops. The exchange format and requirements for the AIM must be included in the EIR. If the employer's software will be able to store the asset information, the EIR should include this. For all but the most experienced of employers, however, the asset information and exchange formats should be decided in conjunction with the project team, either as part of the bid process or between nomination and the finalising of contracts.

According to PAS 1192-2, an information model is the totality of its geometry, information and unchanging documents, and an AIM should be the same. As a number of professions are involved in most construction projects, a number of systems will normally make up this information model; there is unlikely to be one software system that can accommodate all the information before export into the employer's own system. The delivery strategy should therefore be generated with input from the entire project team. Bidding teams and experienced technology and information managers who understand the requirements for information exchange with their most common collaborators are key. This makes the case for simultaneous or concurrent appointment of the project team, or at least professional consultation to ensure that the specified requirements are proportional to the needs, and achievable.

Commercial

The final section of the EIR gives details of BIM model deliverables, the timing of data drops and definitions of information purposes.

Data drops

A data drop or information exchange is the official handover of information deliverables to the employer. This section of the EIR sets out the timing and purpose of data drops for each stage, aligned to the previously defined project work stages.

The employer's project management processes may have their own project stages for asset procurement that will need to be reflected in the BEP. This information handover should enable the employer to answer the plain language questions they create for each project stage, which inform key decisions such as whether to proceed to the next stage. The BIM Task Group's website gives a sample list of plain language questions for employers.

Client's strategic purposes

The ultimate uses of the information supplied to the employer are defined in this section, probably following the proforma statement from PAS 1192-2 shown in Figure 8.3.

P01 Registration	P06 Assessment and re-use
P02 Use and utilisation	P07 Impacts
P03 Operations	P08 Business case
P04 Maintenance and repair	P09 Security and surveillance
P05 Replacement	P10 Regulation and compliance

Figure 8.3 Clients' strategic purposes proforma

This table demonstrates the employer's required uses of the model following on from its original plan for development. Model ownership will need to be confirmed, either within this section of the EIR or through negotiation, to ensure that information ownership and intellectual property rights are protected. Current best practice is for ownership of the model to stay with the organisation that created the work, the originator. They licence their client to use their content for the purposes described in the contract, usually for the purpose of the contract that the originator has been contracted for. The client is given a licence to use the content that they are supplied with in such a way that the right to use the content can never be taken away from them and they need not pay any further fees for the use of the content once supplied. In other words, the client is granted a licence to use the content that is irrevocable and royalty-free. Furthermore, the client can themselves grant a licence to use the supplied content, so that someone else further down the supply chain or later in the design process can use their content.

This copyright approach exists to protect the client and those producing designs, so that the client can get what they pay for, the project team get paid for what they produce and the produced designs are only used for their intended purposes.

BIM-specific competence assessment

This part of the EIR tells the bidder what BIM competences they should demonstrate as part of their submission.

A. *BIM capability and experience* assesses the maturity of a practice and its capabilities; a practice will document its experience here and show how they have the expertise or willingness to implement BIM.

Figure 8.4 BIM
competence assessment

Reference	Item	Response
A	BIM capability and experience	Tenderers should include the following detail: • BIM experience – organisational and personnel • BIM capabilities • Outsourced roles
B	Evidence of BIM Execution Planning	Tenderers should include the following detail: • BIM Execution Plans • Lessons learnt
C	Confirmation of BIM toolset	Tenderers should include the detail on procedures aligned with core project stages as follows: • BS 1192 (2007) • PAS 1192-2 (2013) • COBie UK 2012 • Other bespoke processes
D	Details of BIM workload and resourcing	Tenderers should include the following detail: • Resource matrix with level, number, utilisation • Outsourcing details or services etc.
E	Principal supply chain	Tenderers should include the following detail: • Key supply chain partners • Expected outputs • Assessment process

B. *Evidence of BIM Execution Planning* measures a bidder's ability and willingness to collaborate with other project team colleagues. By demonstrating experience of planning software and process workflows for collaboration, a practice can show that they have the pragmatic and collaborative ethos essential for a successful BIM project.

C. *Confirmation of BIM toolset* asks how the pillars of BIM will be implemented. Not every pillar will be needed on a project, so identifying which standards are proposed for implementation demonstrates the capability to adapt the requirements of BIM to different projects.

D. *Details of BIM workload and resourcing* ensures that the bidder is able to apply the appropriate resources to a given task. This declaration enables an employer to assess a bidder's ability to meet their responsibilities.

E. *Principal supply chain* assesses how the bidder will collaborate with the supply chain both above and below them in the BIM Level 2 tiers. A supply chain that can share information effectively is a requisite for effective information exchange, developing a PIM (Project Information Model) into an AIM (Asset Information Model).

File types

This section of the EIR details the file types required to work with the employer's systems. The employer may have further requirements for information structuring to conform to their in-house standards, such as naming objects within a database, or spreadsheet formats that reflect project stages. This is not the place to define the outputs required throughout the project, unless there is an established business reason to do so; for example, if the design team have to use the same software as the employer's in-house designers, or if file exchange will be through IFC.

References

BSI (2007) *BS 1192:2007 Collaborative production of architectural, engineering and construction information. Code of practice.* London: British Standards Institution.

BSI (2013) *PAS 1192-2:2013 Specification for information management for the capital/delivery phase of assets using Building Information Modelling.* London: British Standards Institution.

BSI (2014a) *PAS 1192-3:2014 Specification for information management for the operational phase of assets using Building Information Modelling.* London: British Standards Institution.

BSI (2014b) *BS 1192-4:2014 Collaborative production of information Part 4: Fulfilling employer's information exchange requirements using COBie. Code of practice.* London: British Standards Institution.

BSI (2015) *PAS 1192-5:2015 Specification for security-minded building information modelling, digital built environments and smart asset management.* London: British Standards Institution.

CIC (2013) *Building Information Model (BIM) Protocol: Standard Protocol for use in projects using Building Information Models.* London: Construction Industry Council.

Construction (Design and Management) Regulations 2015 (SI 2015/51)

Government Soft Landings (2013) *Government Soft Landings micro-site.* London: Department for Business, Innovation and Skills. www.bimtaskgroup.org/gsl

NBS (2015a) *BIM Toolkit.* Newcastle upon Tyne: RIBA Enterprises. https://toolkit.thenbs.com

NBS (2015b) *Uniclass 2015.* Newcastle upon Tyne: RIBA Enterprises. https://toolkit.thenbs.com/articles/classification

CHAPTER 9

Pre-contract

Introduction

This chapter shows how a team prepares to bid by creating a pre-contract BEP in response to the EIR. It looks at the purpose of the BEP and its specific requirements for managing information, enabling collaborative working and providing the right team for the job. It then goes on to look at the creation of a practice's own generic BEP.

BIM's benefits can start to be seen at this early stage, as bidders gain an understanding of future collaborators and project team members. There is also much that can be prepared in advance to meets the needs of PAS 91(BSI, 2013), the standard for construction prequalification questionnaires, or PQQs. Processes and workflows should be largely agreed prior to work beginning, with pre-commencement documentation in place to ensure that consultants understand the employer's information and technical requirements, and those of other consultants. This provides the opportunity for testing and negotiation, and the chance to learn lessons and improve. It is therefore essential that landscape professionals, and in particular technical specialists within landscape practices, are engaged at the earliest possible stages of BIM planning in order to ensure that the feasibility of BIM workflows is correctly assessed.

Purpose of the BEP

A BEP exists in two distinct phases. In its first iteration, pre-contract, it proposes the project team's response to the EIR. Upon appointment, the successful bid team updates this to a post-contract BEP, forming a comprehensive management document describing how BIM will be run on a project, which goes on to form contractual requirements. The second phase is covered in Chapter 10.

The BEP sets out how the team's information management approach would meet the necessary standards and function in the project environment, and should respond to each of the requirements of the EIR. The BEP is also a monitoring tool, defining much of the intention, process and outcomes of the planned workflows. Although its contents may be tightly controlled in order to form the basis of a contractually binding response to the EIR, it can nonetheless facilitate effective information management and information exchange on a project. A BEP helps a project team agree on ways to work with information, respond to others' information needs

Figure 9.1
Employer's pre-project
decision-making process

and get the right type and amount of information themselves (Figure 9.1). This helps create a project environment where guess-work rarely features in decision-making.

Pre-contract BEP

The pre-contract BEP is an initial response to the EIR; it is not the final version, and has fewer requirements than the post-contract version. It includes:

- a Project Implementation Plan (PIP), also known as a supply chain capability summary
- project goals for collaboration and information modelling
- project milestones
- a Project Information Model (PIM) delivery strategy

The employer will judge the BEP against the major criteria of capability, capacity and approach. Capability and capacity responses can be drafted separately by individual practices and then brought together, but the approach should be produced as a team strategy.

The Project Implementation Plan (PIP)

The PIP demonstrates the bidder's BIM capabilities and overall approach to BIM. As different practices manage BIM projects in different ways, the PIP helps the employer choose an appropriate team on the basis of their submission. The PIP gives a standardised outline of capability at the pre-contract stage, and evolves to provide details of resourcing specifics during the project in the post-contract BEP. It should cover human resources, IT support and an indication of the experience and understanding of BIM within the practice. Standardised forms for this purpose are available from the Construction Project Information Committee website (www.cpic.org.uk/cpix), or a bespoke assessment form may be used.

Supply chain capability summary

When teams come together to prepare a response to a brief, each member of the project team provides their own assessment forms that are then summarised by the Information Manager or other appropriate professional within the project bid team. Each proposed task team within the larger project team must submit a PIP, consisting of just the supply chain capability summary at this point. The team should show that they can supply the right level of staffing for the project. It should indicate the core team, and show, for example, how absences will be managed. This can be standardised across the practices that make up the team, but in most instances it will include specific policies and plans for each practice.

Human resources

The project bid team should be created with the right competencies to meet the needs of the project in mind – and with a plan in place to fill any capability gaps. This requirement is not a new one, of course. However, team approach, in terms of culture and attitude to BIM, can be as important as capability; the prequalification process requires a demonstration of a positive and BIM-ready ethos within a practice. Members of the project team will not all have the same levels of BIM knowledge but a bid can be successful with a reasonable training plan in place for a team with varying experience; existing full capability is not necessarily essential. A Resource Assessment form can be used in the team selection process. If an in-house BEP already exists, this should inform specifics for a project, demonstrating the availability of appropriate team members to perform the tasks required on the project within the time frame specified by the employer.

Team hierarchy

The PIP should set out authority for decisions within the practice, either by role or by individual. A Responsibility, Authority, Consultation and Inform (RACI) table could be used (see Figure 9.2 for an example), or a flowchart indicating responsibilities within the project team.

Task	Landscape Architect	Civil Engineer	Hydraulic Engineer	Geotechnical Engineer	Lead Designer
Sustainable Drainage Scheme	A	C	R	C	I
Parking layout	A	R	I	I	C
Key: R – Responsible: has responsibility for producing the output A – Accountable: has overall responsibility for ensuring the work is done and the output delivered C – Consulted: must include their professional opinion in discussions I – Informed: must be updated with progress					

Figure 9.2 A RACI table provides a more nuanced allocation of responsibility

BIM responsibility

The roles of Task Team Manager, Interface Manager and Information Manager must be assigned within each task team, along with the BIM Authors who will generate the models. The Task Team Manager will be responsible for the activities of the task team, the Interface Manager will be responsible for spatial and technical interface resolution, and the Information Manager will be responsible for compliance with the project's information standards. It should be stressed that an individual may perform more than one role. The BIM assessment process, prescribed by BIM Level 2 standards, is intended to ensure that project team members are competent and capable in BIM; the use of a standardised form issued by the employer enables a comparison between bids.

Team roster

This should capture team members' current capabilities, as shown in the example in Figure 9.3.

Team member	Project role(s)	BIM role(s)	Competencies
G. Loci	Project landscape architect	Project Information Manager; Task Team Information Manager	Software training (internal or accredited) Experience
G. Fingers	Landscape technician	BIM Author	Authoring software (accredited)

Figure 9.3 Recording the team capabilities significantly increases transparency

Skills register

A skills register can effectively monitor progress against team members' targets, as shown in Figure 9.4.

Team member	Target competencies	Current competencies	Competencies
A .Name	Software skill levels Project management skill	Project Information Manager; Task Team Information Manager	Software training (internal or accredited)
G. Loci	Visualisation software Authoring software	BIM Author	Authoring software (certified)

Figure 9.4 Recording and updating the team's professional development demonstrates a commitment to continued improvement

IT resources

This section of the PIP is where the bidder describes their hardware, software and network capabilities, to show the employer that their IT infrastructure meets the project's needs. This could also include, for example, an assurance that team members are able to operate the software, that the system has sufficient bandwidth to work with large files on remote servers and that the latest versions of software are in use, with project team members working with the same versions. Further details of these can be entered in the assessment documents provided by the employer or lead designer as part of the capability assessment process.

Goals for collaboration and information modelling

Collaboration is paramount on BIM projects, requiring a cultural shift in terms of how project teams manage themselves and their approach to their work. The goals for collaboration section of the BEP is intended to capture this requirement, where the team demonstrates not only their approach to collaborative working and information exchange, but also makes the case for the benefits their BIM capabilities could bring. These could include:

• supporting reliable decision-making
• improved communication of design intent
• accurate representation of design performance
• rapid and frequent cost analysis capabilities
• time efficiency generated by using the BS 1192 naming strategy
• enhanced involvement of future users and managers of an asset

Any specific systems to be used for information management across the project will be named in this section. The team should demonstrate an understanding of IT security and the particular security requirements of the project, including a definition of access privileges to the CDE and permissions to view, comment on, upload or download files. The Information Manager will have ultimate control of access privileges.

Project milestones

These should, where possible, conform to the employer's project milestones set out in the EIR, as defined by the project management system in place. Work stages, information exchange points, employer's decisions points and data drops should all correlate with the project milestones, unless circumstances dictate otherwise, and these milestones should form the interface between the project and the information management documents.

Project Information Model (PIM) delivery strategy

How will the bid team produce the geometric data, the information describing this data and the documents associated with these datasets that together form the PIM? The PIM delivery strategy section of the BEP defines how the team will create this content and ensure that the information can be used for purposes such as clash detection, costing and phasing. The stages at which project team members will have responsibilities are defined in conjunction with the BIM Toolkit and the project milestones. Figure 9.5 shows an example table.

Project stage: Concept design		
Deliverable/Task	**Software process**	**Interoperability strategy**
Topography – Concept	Topography software guide Located on the network at X:\...	
Cut and fill	Cut and fill software guide Located on the network at X:\...	
Visualisation of topography	Export to visualisation software Located on the network at X:\	Topography to render guide Located on the network at X:\
Project stage: Detailed design		
Deliverable/Task	**Software process**	**Interoperability strategy**
Topography – Concept	Topography software guide Located on the network at X:\...	
Cut and fill	Cut and fill software guide Located on the network at X:\...	
Visualisation of topography	Export to visualisation software Located on the network at X:\	Topography to render guide Located on the network at X:\
Project stage: Construction		
Deliverable/Task	**Software process**	**Interoperability strategy**
Topography – Concept	Topography software guide Located on the network at X:\...	
Cut and fill	Cut and fill software guide Located on the network at X:\...	
Visualisation of topography	Export to visualisation software Located on the network at X:\	Topography to render guide Located on the network at X:\

Figure 9.5 Mapping the process documents for a project creates an unambiguous set of digital workflows

Interoperability strategy

Sharing information between packages requires discussion during the creation of the BEP. It is important that the bid team understands what information can be produced and how, before engaging with other professionals as to timings. The delivery of COBie (Construction Operations Building information exchange, the standardised information exchange protocol) will also need to be discussed. If there is a clear requirement for COBie throughout the project life cycle and operational phase, for example, on central government procured projects, it should be used. If it is not mandated, or if the COBie will not capture all the relevant information, an alternative mechanism for information exchange should be agreed. (Chapter 11 looks at the limitations of COBie in respect to landscape.)

Not every aspect of information exchange capability can be defined at this stage; it is an evolving task that depends on other consultants' software as well as that used within the employer's organisation and the project team. Interoperability issues should be highlighted from the start, however; attempting to bridge gaps that cannot be bridged later in the project can be avoided if constraints are included in the interoperability strategy.

Generic BEP

A BEP responds to an EIR and demonstrates the bidding practice's technical competencies and approach to training and staff development. A generic BEP document includes as a minimum:

- a basic PIP
- the practice's Standard Methods and Procedures
- a menu for developing the PIM

A practice can draft a master generic BEP, from which elements can be taken and released into the public domain as needs be, as information for prospective project teams or to clarify processes, for example. The BEP contains valuable information and using it solely as a project document does not maximise its potential; it can be used in many other ways. A generic BEP may be submitted at prequalification, or information in it used to complete relevant PQQs sections. A practice can also use a generic BEP to review progress against its BIM Implementation Plan. Practices will differ in how much they choose to make public, but as a collaborative process, BIM promotes information sharing, which benefits all concerned. Regardless, the creation of a generic BEP is an important part of any practice's BIM journey.

The contents of the generic BEP fall into two categories: information required for a pre-contract BEP, and information that may or may not be made public. The bid team may decide to put more detail into the first category than they would display to a wider audience; alternatively they may decide that openness is important and share their processes publicly. A generic BEP cannot be specific about exact team rosters, so it should document the entire team and identify capabilities, potential roles and areas for improvement. The result is a generic project team, with an indication of how these capabilities could come together to deliver a project.

Prequalifying with PAS 91

Prequalification processes that follow PAS 91 PQQ standards now include BIM questions. There are exemptions from some sections for practices with a BIM business accreditation, which demonstrates competency in BIM Level 2. Otherwise, a PQQ will require a response to the following BIM-specific elements:

- Ability to use a CDE in an efficient and collaborative manner; a construction-specific and project-specific CDE is the preference.
- Policy systems and procedures to achieve BIM Level 2, signed off by the practice's management, and regularly reviewed. This applies to large and small projects alike.
- Ability to work to a BEP; creating and regularly reviewing a BEP will help demonstrate this criterion.
- BIM training that is planned and assessed demonstrates a commitment to process and technological improvement essential to any BIM Implementation Plan.

Reference

BSI (2013) *PAS 91:2013 Construction prequalification questionnaires.* London: British Standards Institution.

CHAPTER 10

Post-contract BIM Execution Plan

Introduction

After responding to the requirements of the EIR in the pre-contract BEP, the appointed project team will develop a post-contract BEP to define how BIM processes will actually operate. The post-contract BEP shows how their approach will conform to the BIM Level 2 standards, and gives details of the negotiated processes for delivering BIM. When finalised, this becomes an active project management document that develops as the project progresses (Figure 10.1).

Purpose of the post-contract BEP

The post-contract-award BEP is a project-specific document that describes how the appointed team will plan and manage information delivery, and sets out their standards for the execution of the project. Elements of this BEP can be incorporated into an updated EIR, either replacing or supplementing the initial requirements, to maintain a connection between the two documents. The Information Manager, lead designer

Figure 10.1 An overview of how the collaborative process develops in a BIM Level 2 project

Stage	Collaboration	Common Data Environment	EIR	BEP
In house standards	Lessons learnt			
Pre-qualification	Statement of capability		Initial development	
Pre-contract	Initial collaboration process planning		Issued to prospective teams	Respond to initial EIR
Post-contract	Detail process planning	Solution chosen and prepared	Updated in response to BEP as required	
Stage commencement	Processes agreed	CDE initialised	Reviewed as necessary	Reviewed as necessary
Stage execution	Sharing files to CDE for collaboration		Static	Processes followed
Stage completion	Formal handovers of files		Reviewed as necessary	Reviewed as necessary
Project handover	Graduated handover			

and project manager are responsible for the overall content of the BEP, and in order for it to become an effective collaboration tool, they should consult and take advice from the project team as much as possible. Once the contract is awarded, the EIR that formed Appendix 2 to the BIM Protocol (CIC, 2013) becomes a contractual obligation.

The Project Delivery Manager (PDM) needs to ensure that the project team's BEP is up to date and accommodates any changes to the arrangement of the team before commencement. At the project induction meeting the task teams will need to confirm that they have the appropriate staffing in place and are available at the required times. They will also confirm how information will be delivered and the exchange formats to be used. The team should provide the employer with an updated version of the pre-contract BEP's PIP with information on the availability of resources for the allotted tasks within the project.

Requirements of the post-contract BEP

The primary EIR created by the overall employer is used by the team directly responsible to this employer. When there is little subcontracting or contractual hierarchy, the post-contract BEP will respond directly to the main employer's EIR. If there are multiple tiers of procurement, each employer produces an EIR to which subcontracting parties must respond with a BEP (see Figure 10.2). Each post-contract BEP is therefore responsible to the EIR of the contracting party, who in turn creates a BEP in response to their employer's EIR, and so on. These requirements are additional to project brief requirements. At the furthest tier, an EIR may be extremely simple; for example, a contractor wishing to supply trees to site will issue an EIR to a nursery asking for the product information in a given format, with no other requirements.

As the information management document for the project, the BEP details how the team will provide the information required in the EIR. This is set out in the BEP under the main headings of management, planning and documentation, Standard Methods and Procedures, and IT, which are covered in detail in the rest of this chapter. Each project team member may receive their own EIR that responds directly

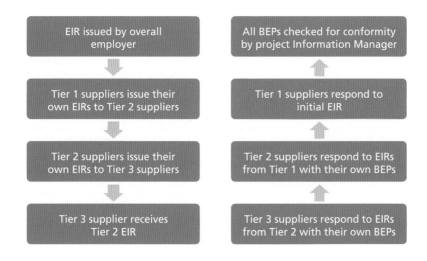

Figure 10.2 An EIR is produced for each tier, to which the subcontracting party responds with a BEP

to their need to supply information, so an arboriculturist will not be given the same information requirements as an ecologist, for instance.

Management

The management section covers:

- roles, responsibilities and authorities
- milestones
- delivery strategy
- survey strategy
- legacy data use
- approval of information
- PIM authorisation process

Roles, responsibilities and authorities

The specific information management roles within the project team and each task team are detailed in this section of the BEP. A Responsibilities, Authorities, Consultation and Inform (RACI) table may be used to define the activities and correspondence required on the project.

Milestones

This section sets the programme's major project milestones and the PIM delivery strategy. The milestones should be drawn from the project management programme or the Master Information Delivery Plan (see Master Information Delivery Plan section); they will be different for each project, determined by the project management practices in place.

Delivery strategy

As specified in PAS 1192-2:2013 (BSI, 2013), the Project Delivery Manager will provide a strategy for the management of information delivery during the project, the management of the federated model, which combines a number of models for review, and the production of project outputs.

Survey strategy

If the employer has their own specific survey strategy, it will be defined in the EIR, otherwise it can be added to the post-contract BEP. The strategy should have input from the entire project team, if possible; the BEP should emphasise that early input from the external works team reduces the need for further surveys to cover external works designers' and engineers' specialist areas. An Ordnance Survey dataset can be used to generate much of the site context, but the information is not always at a suitable resolution for design decisions.

All surveys should be available with 3D data, including both the raw survey data and the data that has been refined by a surveyor. These files will be used by different disciplines, so file formats that all consultants can use should be specified. The project team should agree a format, position within the CDE, and content, which will form the basis of the project team survey strategy.

Legacy data use

This section of the BEP notes the use of any information created by the employer or consultants prior to the commencement of the project; for example, existing data on a facility, or specific products that the employer wishes to reuse. Legacy data must be analysed for accuracy and consistency, in terms of how closely it describes physical objects, and whether it describes every instance of an object, or the object in its entirety. This may be done by the lead designer, surveyor or any consultant with relevant specialist knowledge. If data is missing from a site soil survey, for instance, this can be described and allowance made; information critical to the success of the project would need to be collected again, however. This may be especially true in cases of contamination where legacy information exists, but a comprehensive picture of the site's actual contamination does not.

Approval of information

This section describes each task team's process for managing the approval of information to share with the wider team, which should use the suitability codes in PAS 1192-2:2013 (see page 87).

PIM authorisation process

The project team sets out in this section how they will handle data drops and completed stages of the project. This should be defined in conjunction with the employer and the GSL Champion.

Planning and documentation

The planning and documentation section covers:

- revised PIP
- agreed processes for collaboration and modelling
- agreed matrix of responsibilities
- Information Delivery Plan
- MIDP (Master Information Delivery Plan)
- TIDPs (Task Information Delivery Plans)

Revised PIP

The project team will provide a revised PIP with the staffing plan and specific capabilities for the project. This should include details of how information will be produced, in conjunction with the BIM Toolkit, showing the tasks that will be done, the LoD and the staff responsible.

Agreed processes for collaboration and modelling

The Information Manager will need to include a methodology describing the collective approach of the project team to collaboration and modelling; the agreed processes and/or tables filled out in the pre-contact BEP can be copied and updated if necessary. It also covers any requirements such as the inclusion of specific object types, attribute data, specification information or other information useful for the delivery of the employer's strategic purposes.

Agreed matrix of responsibilities

The responsibilities matrix defines who models what in the BIM and to what Level of Detail. This will include the details given in the Information Delivery Plans and other BIM Level 2 responsibilities, such as the Project Delivery Manager, lead designer and Information Manager, as well as the BIM roles for each task team including Task Team Manager, Information Manager, Interface Manager and BIM Authors.

Information Delivery Plan

An Information Delivery Plan describes how the information required to generate deliverables will be created and exchanged (Figure 10.3). This is in addition to the existing planning of deliverables and tasks on a project as required by the project management approach in place. An Information Delivery Plan should detail the relationships between the information that will be delivered on the project and the tasks that are defined in the wider project management strategy. For instance:

- What deliverables are being produced?
- What information is required to generate this deliverable? Who generates it?
- Who is using this deliverable to provide their own deliverables and what do they need?

Author	Deliverable	Deliverable stage	Protocols
Landscape Architect	Landscape specification	Concept	Project standard 1 BS 1192-2:2013
Landscape Architect	Landscape model	Concept	Project standard 1 BS 1192-2:2013

Figure 10.3 An example Information Delivery Plan layout; each project team will develop its own, to work with its project management processes

Master Information Delivery Plan (MIDP)

The MIDP shows who will be working on which stages and the deliverables they will produce. These deliverables are assigned a LoD for the entire model, so the deliverables produced must be suitable for the purposes of that LoD. The MIDP and associated TIDPs are the responsibility of the Project Delivery Manager. The MIDP will also set out the protocols and processes to which the deliverables will align, which may include project-specific as well as industry-wide standards.

Task Information Delivery Plans (TIDPs)

Each task team produces a TIDP. A large array of task teams will have a hierarchy of Information Delivery Plans, rather than each replicating the same documentation. For instance, a task team responsible for the aesthetics and structure of a sculpted earthwork might consist of a structural engineer, a civil engineer and a landscape architect. Their TIDP will refer mainly to the structural, civil and landscape Information Delivery Plans, only adding processes which are not mentioned elsewhere.

Standard Methods and Procedures

The Standard Methods and Procedures (SMP) for a BIM Level 2 project covers a number of practices that should be standardised or at least coordinated across teams. This section covers:

- volume strategy
- origin and orientation
- naming strategy
- layer naming convention
- construction tolerances
- drawing sheet templates
- annotations, dimensions, abbreviations and symbols
- attribute data

Volume strategy

If large models are to be used or clashes are to be avoided by granting responsibility for specific areas to one consultant, this should be clearly defined.

Origin and orientation

A spatial coordination process should be put in place to provide all team members with an agreed set of spatial coordinates and grid references across each of their software packages. This preparation will pay dividends when loading files from other consultants. Details of the spatial coordination of the project should be established, and the origin point of the project should be confirmed as accurate.

Tests should be undertaken to ensure that survey data can be reliably used in all software packages. It is important that survey information is not exported when files are exported. Other factors that could affect information sharing are scale, the units used, true north and project north (the base files for all work streams should be orientated towards true north when sharing). There are many geospatial coordinates systems (GCS) in use, providing Northings and Eastings or X and Y coordinates with a height above sea level. The GCS must be consistent with the survey data and survey point. Once this base data is in place across the project team, processes will be needed for consultants who do not work to true north or use different coordinates systems, to ensure that the work they upload to the CDE is normalised against the agreed coordinate system and origin point.

Naming strategy

The naming of files, objects within those files and version control should be implemented as per BS 1192:2007 (BSI, 2007) and PAS 1192-2:2013. For file naming and revisions according to the BIM Level 2 standard see BIP 2207 (BSI, 2010: 47–68). Consultants may prefer to show competency in the Level 2 standard but use their practice's own internal naming strategy, or decide to change their naming strategy to match the standard. The naming strategy applies to every level of a file used in a project, from the name of the file and its version, to the names of layers, objects, groups, components, blocks and families. Files uploaded to a CDE require suitability codes (found in Table 3 of PAS 1192-2:2013) to indicate the uses to which they can be put (see page 87).

Layer naming convention

If file naming and layer naming conventions differ from BS 1192:2007, this should be specified either within the BEP or with a referring document. The requirement to work to a common template means that project team members will need to amend their in-house layer naming conventions to suit. It is advisable for consultants to be flexible in terms of adapting to new conventions.

Construction tolerances

Tolerances within landscape, particularly soft landscape, are less stringent than in other areas; consultants in other professions working in the same area may require an increase in tolerance in some cases, however. Disciplines should operate within their own tolerance requirements and ensure that these are communicated to the rest of the project team.

Drawing sheet templates

Standardised drawing sheets give greater consistency across projects where a high level of standardisation is required. The BEP can give details of templates and where they can be accessed within the CDE.

Annotations, dimensions, abbreviations and symbols

Units of measurement must be supplied to the Information Manager to ensure the required level of consistency across the project deliverables, and interoperability of different consultants' models.

Attribute data

Attributes are the properties or characteristics that define an asset, facility, zone, object or space on a project, such as a BREEAM rating or its specification. A BIM Level 2 project is required to include COBie data as a form of information exchange. In order to populate this information exchange file, steps should be taken to ensure that the information required within the COBie can be extracted from the model files or specification, and updated to reflect changes to the design with minimal manual entry. Plans should be in place to ensure that the attribute data supplied by other members of the task teams is fit for purpose, and compatible with the wider project objectives.

IT solutions

The IT solutions section covers:

- software versions
- exchange formats
- process and data management systems

Software versions

The formats of files produced on the project must be recorded in the BEP, to safeguard against compatibility problems between different versions of software. This information should include the version number as well as any service packs, patches or plug-ins that have been applied.

Exchange formats

The agreed file formats and specific versions used for information exchange are specified here. The Information Manager and project team should undertake an assessment to ensure that the exchange formats facilitate the sharing of information required by the various consultants and meet the needs of the AIM.

Process and data management systems

This section defines the tools that will be used to manage project and model information. Software tools can include the BIM Toolkit for managing LoD, and the DPoW. The CDE should be defined for managing the storage and distribution of model files. These tools are the minimum, but could include enterprise resource planners or other project management tools.

References

BSI (2007) *BS 1192:2007 Collaborative production of architectural, engineering and construction information. Code of practice.* London: British Standards Institution.
BSI (2010) *BIP 2207 Building information management. A standard framework and guide to BS 1192.* London: British Standards Institution.
BSI (2013) *PAS 1192-2:2013 Specification for information management for the capital/delivery phase of assets using Building Information Modelling.* London: British Standards Institution.
CIC (2013) *Building Information Model (BIM) Protocol: Standard Protocol for use in projects using Building Information Models.* London: Construction Industry Council.

CHAPTER 11

Information management

Introduction

Information management is the administration of information on a project. This encompasses the standards to which the information is produced, its ownership, possible uses and distribution. In a built environment project, information consists of models and the graphical and non-graphical information they hold. This chapter covers the application of the key information management standards on a BIM Level 2 project. It also looks at the CDE, the central data store for the project, and the information delivery cycle by which files are approved and shared. Document and information management is key to BIM Level 2. Every stage of a development project is different, but on a BIM Level 2 project there is a common set of processes within every project stage that facilitate good information management.

Information management standards

The standards that comprise the BIM mandate in the UK are still evolving, and increasingly support infrastructure and landscape-based applications of BIM as they develop (Figure 11.1). Readers are reminded that it is essential to check the currency of standards used on a project and to be aware of any changes due.

BS 1192:2007: Collaborative production of architectural, engineering and construction information

BIM Level 2 is underpinned by BS 1192:2007 (BSI, 2007) which, together with its guidebook, BIP 2207 (BSI, 2010), sets out the fundamental requirements for BIM. It covers roles and responsibilities, the CDE, spatial coordination and Standard Methods and Procedures, including file naming, layer naming, suitability codes, and versions and revisions. BS 1192:2007 was under review at the time of writing and it should be noted that much has been updated in PAS 1192-2:2013, in particular that suitability codes have been amended. Neither can its spatial coordination definition be considered an instruction manual for coordination on a project.

Figure 11.1 How the
BIM Level 2 standards
relate to each other

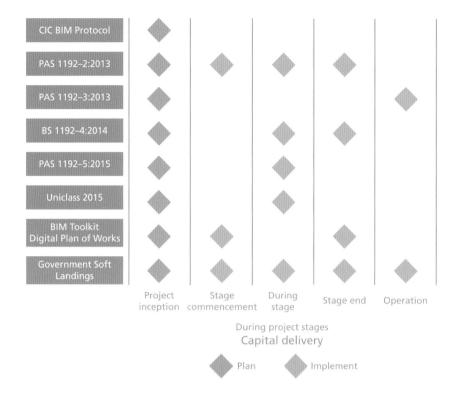

PAS 1192-2:2013: Specification for information management for the capital/delivery phase of assets using Building Information Modelling

This standard (BSI, 2013) provides the project management guide for BIM Level 2. Project team members need a working knowledge of this standard, and it will be the first point of reference for the project's designers. It sets out the BIM Level 2 process timeline, defining how projects operate from inception through to construction and handover. It also details the roles and responsibilities of those involved in the design and construction phase, and covers the creation of pre- and post-contract BEPs in response to an EIR. In terms of information management, it defines the requirement for effective information exchange throughout a project, at commencement, during each project stage, and at the end. The current suitability codes, identifying the reliability of documents in the CDE, can be found in Table 3 of Corrigendum A1 (see page 87).

BS 1192-4:2014: Fulfilling employer's information exchange requirements using COBie – Code of practice

This code of practice (BSI, 2014a) governs the use of COBie as an information exchange tool and specifies how information is to be supplied to the employer. The lead designer or contractor is responsible for providing the employer with documented information about an asset's spatial arrangement and physical attributes, and the standard should therefore be used in consultation with employers, asset managers and facilities managers to enable them to define their requirements. The bare minimum requirement is a COBie handover at the end of the construction process, although it recommends more frequent information exchanges. Landscape practitioners should be aware that COBie is a subset of the IFC, which does not currently include landscape-specific objects. Other documents that describe, for example, the planting or hardworks for a site should therefore be referenced in the COBie and supplied as separate documents; the Landscape Institute's Product Data Templates' (PDTs) data fields can be easily attributed to IFC datasets.

PAS 1192-3:2014: Specification for information management for the operational phase of assets using Building Information Modelling

This document (BSI, 2014b) gives guidance on ensuring that asset managers receive clear, accurate and complete operational information at handover, and how that information should be maintained and used throughout the life cycle of the asset. When a BIM Level 2 project comes to be redeveloped, this standard will guide how that takes place.

The CDE

Central to the BIM Level 2 project is the CDE, the central data store and source of information during the project, housing all the documents that form part of the project's deliverables. The CDE provides a means of sharing information within the project team, both in general and to meet the requirements of particular project stages. The CDE is structured so that files are held in different areas according to their status; each project team member stores work in progress in a dedicated area, which is moved to a shared area when ready, shown in Figure 11.2. Beyond this core functionality, other common features make the CDE a comprehensive project tool, such as 3D modelling of a project with the ability to mark up the model for others to see, as well as more transparent communication within the project team than is offered by email, for instance.

The Information Manager is responsible for the CDE; this role is described in detail in Chapter 12. Amongst other duties, the Information Manager maintains the required standards for information sharing, ensures that software used on the project produces outputs that meet the needs of the EIR, makes sure files are uploaded on schedule, and looks after the system's user permissions and security. The Information Manager decides a structure for project files within the CDE in order to fulfil the requirements of the EIR and the standards defined within it. This includes the file-naming system and CDE internal structure. Only content approved by the Task Team Manager and Task Team Information Manager may be submitted to the CDE. Data drops and the movement of information from 'work in progress' to 'published' require sign-off by the Information Manager, project manager and/ or the lead designer as appropriate. File-naming protocol and metadata can identify information about, for example, intellectual property, responsibility or ownership, and will also describe the uses for which a file is suitable.

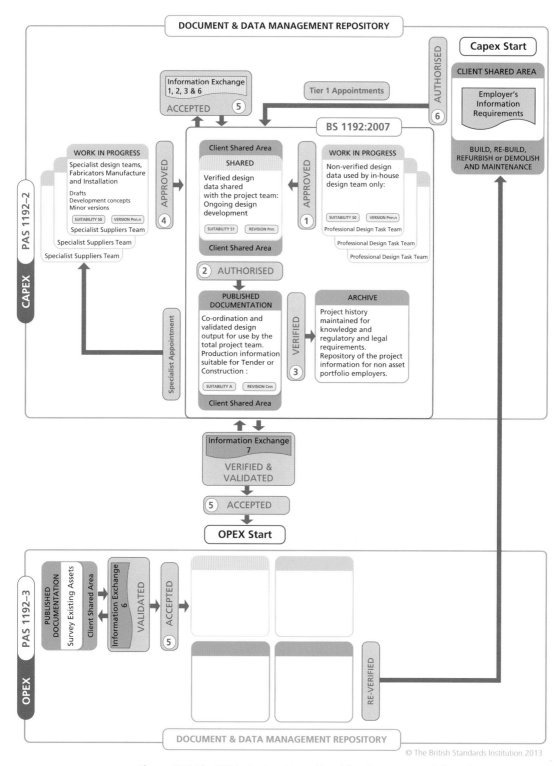

Figure 11.2 The CDE is structured to enable quick and easy access to information

The information delivery cycle

The deliverables for each project stage are developed by and exchanged between project team members. The Information Manager has overall management responsibility for ensuring that information is shared to the CDE correctly by the task teams, and the Task Team Information Managers are responsible for ensuring that their task teams upload files to the CDE correctly. This is the information delivery cycle. The contents of the CDE form the Project Information Model (PIM) during this stage.

When work is ready to be moved into the shared area it must be approved by the Task Team Manager, who will check for suitability for purpose and appropriate technical content, for instance. The Information Manager should check that the project's Standard Methods and Procedures are in place, that the COBie is suitably complete and that any drawings extracted from the models are correctly coordinated. This work may then be shared for reference by other members of the project team.

Figure 11.3 Current suitability codes from PAS 1192-2:2013

Status	Description
Work in Progress (WIP)	
S0	Initial status or WIP Master document index of file identifiers uploaded into the extranet.
Shared	
S1	Issued for co-ordination The file is available to be "shared" and used by other disciplines as a background for their information.
S2	Issued for information
S3	Issued for internal review and comment
S4	Issued for construction approval
S5	Issued for manufacture
S6	Issued for PIM authorization (Information Exchanges 1–3)
S7	Issued for AIM authorization (Information Exchange 6)
D1	Issued for costing
D2	Issued for tender
D3	Issued for contractor design
D4	Issued for manufacture/procurement
AM	As maintained
Published documentation	
A	Issued for construction
B	Partially signed-off: For construction with minor comments from the client. All minor comments should be indicated by the insertion of a cloud and a statement of "in abeyance" until the comment is resolved, then resubmitted for full authorization.
AB	As-built handover documentation, PDF, native models, COBie, etc.

Further uploads of files may be required as the design develops to ensure that the information meets requirements and correlates with the shared files of other professionals on the CDE. At this point the files can be moved to the shared area with the appropriate suitability code (see Figure 11.3). This continues until the project documents reach the appropriate Level of Definition for that stage, whether conceptual or detailed, and the work can then be authorised, represented as moving through gate 2 in Figure 11.2.

This is the critical information exchange or data drop that facilitates and informs the employer's decision point, a key project milestone at the end of a project stage. The employer's representative is responsible for moving these files into the published area, and making sure that the work meets the requirements of the EIR and the employer's plain language questions. When entering the construction phase, the published information will be tested for correlation with the development on site, so that the files can move into the archive section of the CDE. Once the development is complete and verified, the information model becomes known as the Asset Information Model (AIM) as the information that it contains now describes the asset itself. It can then be migrated to a new system.

Questions have sometimes arisen about the copyright and liability implications of work in a shared environment or integrated into a single model. In short, copyright on digital files applies in the same way as it does to paper documents. All fit-for-purpose CDEs clearly indicate which practice or task team has uploaded, downloaded and amended files, so responsibilities for design are clear. Ownership of the information remains with the originator of that information unless the originator assigns the benefit of the copyright. This provides a clear audit trail for the project, protecting the intellectual property of project team members as well as preventing accidental infringements of copyright.

Information delivery stages

PAS 1192-2 follows the CIC work stages. Each project stage has an associated project team information exchange indicated by the status codes. These refer to end-of-stage handovers of project information (Figure 11.4).

Decision-making

Managing the design of a BIM Level 2 construction project requires considerable discussion and agreement. There are many decisions that must be taken, particularly relating to collaborative working and information exchange processes, and it is important that the project team understands the status of these decisions. They can be categorised as standardised, prescribed, negotiated, flexible and unresolved.

Standardised

Standardised decisions in BIM are matters prescribed in the Level 2 standards and apply as a matter of course to the entire project team. This covers, for example, naming standards and suitability codes for issuing files. Where standardised processes are

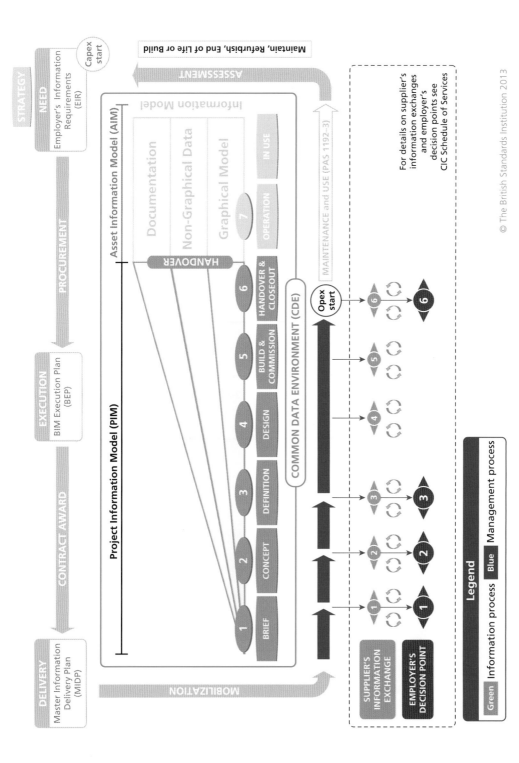

Figure 11.4 The information delivery – production table from PAS 1192-2:2013 defines when information is formally shared, at the end of certain project stages

For details on supplier's information exchanges and employer's decision points see CIC Schedule of Services

Legend

Green Information process | Blue Management process

SUPPLIER'S INFORMATION EXCHANGE

EMPLOYER'S DECISION POINT

COMMON DATA ENVIRONMENT (CDE)

MAINTENANCE and USE (PAS 1192-3)

Opex start

Capex start

Maintain, Refurbish, End of Life or Build

STRATEGY

NEED — Employer's Information Requirements (EIR)

PROCUREMENT

EXECUTION — BIM Execution Plan (BEP)

CONTRACT AWARD

DELIVERY — Master Information Delivery Plan (MIDP)

ASSESSMENT

HANDOVER

MOBILIZATION

Information Model

Asset Information Model (AIM)

Project Information Model (PIM)

Documentation

Non-Graphical Data

Graphical Model

1 BRIEF | 2 CONCEPT | 3 DEFINITION | 4 DESIGN | 5 BUILD & COMMISSION | 6 HANDOVER & CLOSEOUT | 7 OPERATION | IN USE

used, it can simply be stated in the project documents that the project will conform to the standard for the given process. So in a process following the COBie implementation standard to the letter, the project documents need only say that COBie will be generated according to the guidance of BS 1192-4. In order for a standardised approach to be used, the project team should be reasonably confident that the standard covers every possible use case for their project.

Prescribed

Prescribed decisions are those with which the project team must abide in order to fit into some larger scheme, usually compliance with the EIR. Project documents might say, for instance, that schedule information will be produced using the spreadsheet format layout and file type specified within the EIR, as already used by the employer, enabling information to function effectively within the employer's systems when the asset is in use.

Negotiated

Negotiated decisions form the main body of decisions required for a successful BIM project, and often relate to solving common causes of waste on construction projects. Negotiated decisions regarding collaborative working occur when it is agreed that a certain order or cycle of processes should take place for the best resolution of the design. This is particularly important where the professional practices of task teams overlap in scope. Negotiated decisions are where the innovation happens in BIM. The resolutions of challenging situations or long-standing issues are valuable potential benefits from a BIM project, and it is through negotiated decisions that the project team can realise these opportunities.

Flexible

Flexible decisions are those that can change without impacting the outcomes of the project.

Unresolved

There will always be aspects of a project that are unknown at the time of writing the project documents. Rather than attempting to prejudge outcomes or deal with issues that cannot be dealt with at the time, these issues may be highlighted as unresolved, with a next action against them to be revisited in due course.

References

BSI (2007) *BS 1192:2007 Collaborative production of architectural, engineering and construction information. Code of practice.* London: British Standards Institution.
BSI (2010) *BIP 2207 Building information management. A standard framework and guide to BS 1192.* London: British Standards Institution.

BSI (2013) *PAS 1192-2:2013 Specification for information management for the capital/ delivery phase of assets using Building Information Modelling.* London: British Standards Institution.

BSI (2014a) *BS 1192-4:2014 Collaborative production of information Part 4: Fulfilling employers' information exchange requirements using COBie. Code of practice.* London: British Standards Institution.

BSI (2014b) *PAS 1192-3:2014 Specification for information management for the operational phase of assets using Building Information Modelling.* London: British Standards Institution

CHAPTER 12

Role responsibilities

Introduction

The BIM standards define roles for every professional engaged in the design of a project, and create two new key roles – the Information Manager and the Interface Manager, introduced in Chapter 6. This chapter now looks in detail at the responsibilities accompanying these roles, and their contribution to managing information flows and coordinating technical overlaps. It also introduces the role of task teams, the project sub-teams that help enable collaboration across professional and organisational boundaries.

A number of current roles within the built environment sector are given specific names within the BIM Level 2 standards (see Figure 12.1). Project team and task team are the two main groups. The project team refers to the entire team responsible for delivering the project; roles with 'project' in the title have responsibilities across the entire project. Task teams are teams with a particular responsibility; this may be the traditional responsibility of one consultant or a single-discipline team within an organisation, but could apply equally to collocated teams of multiple disciplines.

PAS 1192-2 title	Also known as
Project Delivery Manager	Project Manager
Lead Designer	Design Lead Lead Consultant Principal Designer
Information Originator/BIM Author	Landscape Architect Designer Architect Engineer Technician
Task Team Manager	Consultant Project Lead
Interface Manager (new role)	BIM Manager BIM Coordinator
Information Manager (new role)	BIM Manager BIM Coordinator

Figure 12.1 BIM Level 2 roles as they may otherwise be known

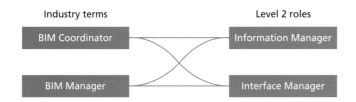

Industry terms — Level 2 roles

BIM Coordinator — Information Manager

BIM Manager — Interface Manager

Figure 12.2 BIM roles and their potential overlaps

The Information Manager

The Information Manager ensures that effective information exchanges take place, and is the gatekeeper and guardian of the CDE (Figure 12.2). As the lead Information Manager, this role is ultimately responsible for the information delivered on the project, that is, every project working file, output or deliverable. Deciding whether information or designs are right or wrong is not within the remit of the role; the Information Manager is responsible only for ensuring that the correct files are present and conform to the project standards – the team members who produce the files are responsible for their contents.

The Information Manager standards

PAS 1192-2 and the BIM Protocol (CIC, 2013a) require the appointment of an Information Manager to the project. The outline scope of services for information management published by the Construction Industry Council (CIC, 2013b) is the primary guidance on embedding information management within a project, filling the gap between PAS 1192-2:2013 and BS 1192:2007 which define the role loosely (BSI, 2013, 2007). The specifics of the role will need to be agreed by the employer and project team for each project, including decisions as to the appointee, their responsibilities and the scope of services.

Who takes the role of Information Manager?

An already appointed professional such as the design coordination manager or project manager could take on this role. As the role does not require design or engineering competency, the Information Manager could also be an IT professional, experienced in managing technology, people and deadlines. Alternatively, an independent Information Manager could be appointed. An independent appointee can have the advantage of serving the overall needs of the project impartially; it may also be preferable to use an independent specialist rather than inexperienced project team members to cover duties. As an independent Information Manager can be procured separately, their involvement can be more closely managed by the employer for greater cost efficiency.

Some practices currently employ roles that carry much of the responsibility of an Information Manager under another name, or sometimes responsibilities are shared amongst members of the project team. Where this is the case, it should be clarified whether the duties of the Information Manager as specified in the standards are fulfilled, namely responsibility for the management of information project-wide and within each task team. In this way, even if the BIM standards' naming conventions are not used, a project can still be described as BIM Level 2. In any case, the information management tasks should be contractually defined to avoid confusion or doubt.

Information Manager scope of services

This description of the Information Manager's role is based on PAS 1192-2 and the CIC scope of services, which specify three core responsibilities:

- managing the CDE
- project information management
- collaborative working, information exchange and project team management

Managing the CDE

The Information Manager's gatekeeping role involves setting up protocols to receive files into the information model defined in the EIR. (The information model in this context refers to the entirety of information produced for the project: documents, databases, spreadsheets and models.) The Information Manager maintains the standards of data integrity required by the EIR, and manages access and security policies so that only authorised users can log in, or add or delete files where needed, for instance.

The Information Manager is ultimately responsible for the file handling on the project, and collaborates with the project team to agree standards for this. As CDE gatekeeper, the Information Manager will ask for submitted work that does not meet the agreed requirements to be amended and resubmitted. They are also responsible for moving files between different areas of the CDE as they develop. The Information Manager will accept changes authorised by the Task Team Manager if a file is named and structured according to the project standards; it is the responsibility of the lead designer or Project Delivery Manager to check that the information that it contains is correct.

Project information management

The Information Manager is responsible for setting up the project-wide standards for information deliverables. They have a number of information management tools at their disposal. The core BIM Level 2 tools are the TIDPs produced by task teams, discussed in Chapter 10, which together form the MIDP. These documents set out the protocols and information deliverables for each task team, enabling the definition of task teams' responsibilities. Depending on the standards in place, the Information Manager may also develop Project Information Plans and Asset Information Plans (AIPs). At the time of writing, both the PIP and AIPs are similar in intent to TIDPs and the MIDP, but are not referenced outside the CIC scope of services document.

Information structure

The Information Manager implements an information structure based on the appointed project team's BEP, to which consultants must conform, although the agreed standards may change as the project develops. The Information Manager then ensures that task teams meet their upload deadlines according to the project milestones.

Level of Definition

The Information Manager has responsibility for ensuring that the agreed Level of Definition for each stage on the project is properly filled out; the BIM Toolkit can be used for this (see toolkit.thenbs.com for guidance). The appointed consultants should demonstrate that they meet the information requirements of the project by developing the appropriate models to the correct LoD for the corresponding stage, as defined within the project brief and according to the project milestones.

Format of outputs

Project information management covers the standardisation of design coordination and production. The Information Manager's responsibility for the format of outputs begins with a consideration of the designed outputs required to serve the needs of the project team, the employer, the construction team and those responsible for maintaining and managing the asset after completion. The choice of file formats used by the project team generally requires considerable care, given software inter-operability issues across the built environment sector. Landscape consultants may need to consider alternative methods for design coordination, as the IFC standard is not yet fully applicable beyond the building envelope; the Landscape Institute's PDTs' properties sets can form the standard for landscape work, and can be applied to IFC standard (see Chapter 15 for more on PDTs).

Collaborative working, information exchange and project team management

Updating Appendix 1 and 2 of the BIM Protocol

The appendices of the BIM Protocol give contractual status to BIM implementation on a project. Appendix 1 requires the Information Manager to update the respon-sibilities matrix in line with the contents of the BIM Toolkit, describing responsibility for tasks and deliverables at each stage of the project, including Level of Definition where appropriate. The EIR constitutes Appendix 2. The implementation of the BIM Protocol is vital to the correct execution of a BIM Level 2 project; without it the project documents carry little legal weight.

Support collaborative culture

The Information Manager fosters effective collaboration between consultants, so that project team members find the working environment beneficial both to themselves professionally and to the project. Team members looking for a particular piece of information, or members of the employer's team with queries should make the Information Manager their first port of call.

Organise the project team's information exchange meetings

The Information Manager assists project team members in establishing information exchange processes, including defining and agreeing procedures for convening, chairing, and recording information exchange process meetings.

Project management responsibilities

This area of responsibility requires participation in and compliance with project team management procedures and processes, including:

- risk and value management
- performance management and measurement procedures
- change management procedures including adjustments to budgets and programme
- attendance at project and design team meetings as required
- implementing record keeping, archiving and an audit trail for the information model

Security

The security of the CDE is one of the Information Manager's primary responsibilities. Protocols will vary depending on the nature of the CDE and the employer's security requirements defined in the EIR. Security measures will be largely handled by the provider where a CDE is hosted by a dedicated external service, but the Information Manager will still need the project team to observe security protocols as the project demands. This covers, for example, protecting the intellectual property of the employer and the team, safeguarding files from deletion, corruption, unauthorised copying or unauthorised editing, and ensuring that all activities taking place within the CDE are documented for transparency.

Data integrity

The Information Manager maps the interfaces of all the software in use to make sure that information can be shared, based either on their own knowledge of the software, or in consultation with task teams. Complete and computable data enables the entire project team not only to produce their required outputs, but also to implement innovative practices on the project and perform useful calculations, from micro-climate analysis to costing. Protocols may be required for the employer to manage their information when required, ensuring that suitable access privileges are given to stakeholders.

The Interface Manager

The Interface Manager works with the volume strategy, defining the spatial volumes for which they are responsible, and liaises with the Task Team Interface Managers appointed by the task teams. According to the standards, an Interface Manager deals purely with the spatial coordination of a construction design. In practice, however, the role sometimes manages some of the technical interactions between design disciplines as well. The strategy for managing interfaces will be in place from the project outset and can be defined on a project-wide basis or by task team, as required.

In its simplest form, interface management involves a task team interfacing only with directly adjacent volumes, and only then when they have to include design work outside their volume. In many built environment projects, however, several participants will work on an element of a design. For example, a volume might be assigned to an avenue of street trees and collocated services (see Figure 12.3). Sufficient volume must be given to the trees, including the reach of their canopies and root zone at maturity, with implications for underground or other engineering services. This presents an interface between professional teams, and the information that informs this relationship is handled by the Interface Manager. Furthermore, placing a street furniture volume over a services volume will create problems when access is required to the services below. The role of the Interface Manager is to highlight potential clashes to the engineer responsible for the services and the landscape professional responsible for the street furniture, to enable them to resolve the issue; if they are unable to resolve it, the final decision rests with the lead designer.

Complex technical and spatial interfaces still require professional judgement by consultants. In a BIM project, the whole project team can access the information they need, facilitating effective decision-making. It may not be possible to predict how information will be used by every team member, as professional needs differ, but from pre-commencement onwards, measures should be in place to ensure effective information exchange and collaboration from the start.

Timings

Interface management can take place at the project milestones defined from the outset within the EIR and the pre- and post-contract BEP, as well as the TIDPs and the MIDP, or as issues arise (Figure 12.3).

Task teams

Task teams are specialised sub-teams focused on particular outcomes or processes (see Figure 12.4). Task Team Information Managers are appointed by task teams, and report to the project Information Manager. They are responsible for their teams' information management, ensuring compliance with the requirements of the EIR and the post-contract BEP when information from their team is shared on the CDE. This includes responsibility for implementing the protocols and standards that define information deliverables on the project, which may include naming strategies, suitability codes and any other information management tools.

Figure 12.3 The interfaces between designed elements can be complex, requiring input from several consultants. Assigning volumes to designed areas reduces conflicts in design and allocates areas of responsibility.

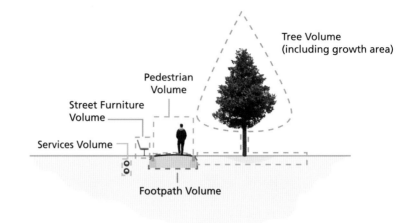

Figure 12.4 Relationship between task teams and the project team

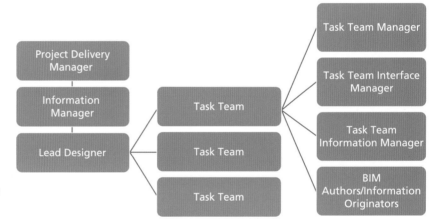

Task Team Interface Managers highlight issues relating to design overlap between their task team and others, which may be technical or spatial in nature. If there is a direct overlap of designed objects, or some technical interface, this will need to be raised with the Interface Manager of the corresponding task team. The interface between task teams depends on the responsibilities of each team, the Interface Managers of these task teams and the protocols for managing such interfaces as defined within the EIR and post-contract BEP.

Task team definition

The project management team and project team decide how to group task teams. The current arrangement involves each separate discipline forming their own task team, but alternative interdisciplinary team structures are increasingly being explored; BS 11000 (BSI, 2010), the collaborative business relationships standard, provides a basis for new collaborative strategies on construction projects, for example.

Task teams can be practically divided into different categories:

- *Volume*
  Bringing together professionals from different disciplines to work on the same volume can overcome technical and spatial design issues, and foster a better understanding of others' perspectives. Volumes may be physical, with responsibilities allocated to a single consultant, or may include multiple elements that require a function-based approach.
- *Phasing*
  Large or complex projects are often divided into phases. Phasing can perpetuate a silo mentality and have a detrimental impact on interoperability and interfaces between phase task teams. Allowing some scope for interaction between task teams outside these phases and across the disciplines can help mitigate these effects, however.
- *System, object or work package*
  Many complex objects require dedicated teams to ensure that the correct expertise is available, especially on infrastructure projects. This is already often the case where overall responsibility is allocated for the provision of sustainable drainage, for example, with other consultants supporting or consulted as necessary, according to their specialisms. Using the example of a sustainable drainage scheme, the landscape architect might have overall design responsibility, with additional responsibility for designing the planting, while the civil engineer works on the engineering aspects.

An overarching ambition for BIM is to erode the traditional silo-based approach in construction that causes waste and fragmentation. Alternative arrangements of responsibilities to the usual hierarchy of professional disciplines can enable professionals to work together more effectively. These approaches can help resolve the issue of design segregation, particularly if project team members are appointed within the same contractual framework and are working towards the same EIR at the same time. Projects where consultants who work together on a given volume or system are appointed at different times may be affected by not having the relevant expertise in place from the outset.

References

BSI (2007) *BS 1192:2007 Collaborative production of architectural, engineering and construction information. Code of practice.* London: British Standards Institution.

BSI (2010) *BS 11000-1:2010 Framework specification for collaborative business relationships.* London: British Standards Institution.

BSI (2013) *PAS 1192-2:2013 Specification for information management for the capital/delivery phase of assets using Building Information Modelling.* London: British Standards Institution.

CIC (2013a) *Building Information Model (BIM) Protocol: Standard Protocol for use in projects using Building Information Models.* London: Construction Industry Council.

CIC (2013b) *Outline scope of services for the role of information management.* London: Construction Industry Council.

CHAPTER 13

Surveys

Introduction

The BEP describes a survey strategy, as seen in Chapter 10, to make sure that the project team has the right information to work with from the start. This chapter now looks at the aspects of site surveys that relate to information delivery and management. Site information is vital to effective decision-making throughout the lifetime of an asset, and surveys are key in a BIM Level 2 project in enabling the lean construction aims of reducing the risk of unplanned costs and delays. BIM does not use different survey techniques, but the data sharing and modelling sophistication involved require a particularly high standard of survey data for maximum accuracy and reliability.

Survey strategy

The site survey is the first digital representation of the physical site seen by the project team (Figure 13.1). More data is added as the project progresses and the need for specialist and more detailed information develops. The team's geomatics engineer will generate the survey strategy, ideally with input from all the disciplines on a project team that need existing assets to be included within their models, to ensure that they receive the correct quality and quantity of information. This information is collated within the live project BEP. Designing the components of an asset only to find they need repositioning later adds time and cost to projects. This is not simply a question of rework, but potentially the re-evaluation of technical decisions, and the risk of needing additional work on site in light of information that was not correctly captured, impacting the constructability of the project. Low-quality information makes wrong decisions far more likely.

Point elevations should be described using 3D point objects to the correct height, with the associated text also at the same elevation. Contour lines should be clearly marked, of a consistent elevation and created from the raw survey data. Creating interpreted contour lines from the data produces a cascade of poor quality; once the surveyor has averaged and simplified the data, so too does the next recipient of the information and so on until it is no longer usable. After examining the full dataset, the landscape consultant should instruct the surveyor to simplify any overly complex geometry to provide only the data required for their work on landscape design, construction and management.

Surveys present significant scope for reducing waste. Lean processes and the leveraging of technology can facilitate more efficient use of site visits and more effective survey techniques, for example, ensuring that the data captured meets requirements. Visits to site should be coordinated to avoid repetition of activities, so that, for example, consultants from different disciplines requiring soil samples can liaise to minimise the number of holes dug and samples taken.

Survey information is converted into a number of different formats to suit the various software packages in use on any built environment project, specified in the PIP and the BEP. Performing this conversion just once before the issue of the survey rather than each office doing their own reduces over-work and ensures consistency. The landscape consultant requires other site surveys such as ecological, arboricultural and soil surveys to add to the information produced by the geomatics surveyor. Lean prescribes that these surveys should not gather information that has already been recorded, such as the heights of buildings or trees, unless they can provide better quality data. Working with the same base dataset throughout the project reduces the probability of errors being introduced to the project by less robust data gathered on subsequent surveys; it should be made clear where survey information is verified site data and where information is inferred.

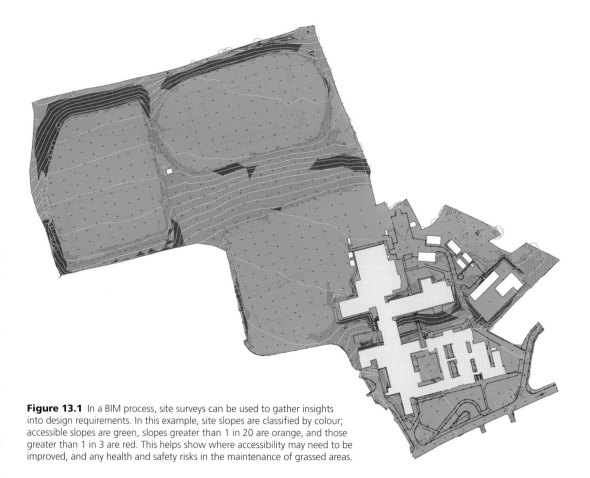

Figure 13.1 In a BIM process, site surveys can be used to gather insights into design requirements. In this example, site slopes are classified by colour; accessible slopes are green, slopes greater than 1 in 20 are orange, and those greater than 1 in 3 are red. This helps show where accessibility may need to be improved, and any health and safety risks in the maintenance of grassed areas.

Surveying techniques

When used in combination with accurate GPS devices, a survey can now be extremely accurate. Survey information is created by a combination of physical tools and software, upon which landscape professionals and all other team members rely. The physical tools are sensors of various types, depending on the scale of the project and accessibility of the site. Regional or national scale projects may use mapping quality information that can be relied upon to an accuracy of several metres. In difficult or dangerous to access sites, unmanned aerial vehicles (drones) or weather balloons can enable a comprehensive survey, although it should be noted that the use of drones is strictly regulated by the Civil Aviation Authority. Otherwise less technologically ambitious but nonetheless effective techniques such as a level and stadia rod will fulfil the requirements. A scanning unit may provide full colour point clouds or spatial coordinates, or may simply register the distance from which a surveyor will have to make their own inferences. Photogrammetry is a developing software-based process for creating visually very high-quality survey data, whereby an object is photographed from a number of angles, enabling a calculation of its dimensions; 3D modelling can then create a virtual object that is dimensionally and visually true to the original. This technique works most readily on smaller objects, although it is possible in the right conditions to capture buildings and other large objects.

Managing survey data

Large datasets

There are usability implications associated with the quantity of data collected during a survey. Every survey requires some processing by the surveyor to make files more manageable and data more comprehensible. Although large datasets may seem the best output, quantity of data does not equal quality – in fact, the opposite may be true. Point clouds, for example, provide exceptionally large and accurate datasets. A point cloud is a set of 3D points recorded by a laser scanning device that can capture levels and surrounding features with great accuracy – but will also include pedestrians, parked cars and low-flying pigeons, while simultaneously failing to record light-reflecting surfaces such as windows and water. The result is a huge but incomplete dataset. A point cloud post-production phase is advisable, transforming the scans into a usable form for the employer and the design team, creating 3D objects with enough embedded data to classify them as assets, and removing extraneous details to allow them to become part of the project team's digital workflows.

Information

Some file formats can generate additional information about objects on site; for instance, defining hard landscape materials. Assuming software compatibility and sufficient use for the information, a modelling process can begin that creates an AIM from the outset. Adding information to the raw survey data can create objects with defined attributes, allowing an understanding of materials in a model, for instance, that creates possibilities such as recycling or thermal calculations. The Information Manager should ensure that information created in this way aligns with the needs of the project, and if it is decided that this information will be added to the survey model, it is important to ensure that it can be used by the whole project team, with no interoperability issues. The Level of Definition for the surveyed objects may be included in the Digital Plan of Works and project BEP to ensure that surveying teams produce information to the appropriate Level of Detail and Level of Information for the given project stage.

Technical surveys

Survey procurement may need to be reviewed, to ensure that surveys gather the data required for use in a BIM workflow. Trees, wildlife and structures above ground will require surveying after the initial survey; geological, geotechnical or hydrological surveys may also be necessary. Surveyors should ensure that there is no ambiguity in the base survey that they use, as this provides the foundation for later surveys that provide new information. Technical surveys inform a BIM workflow from the outset; the graphical information defining the positions of objects and the metadata that describes them must be closely linked and in a digital format.

Project teams should therefore ensure that the information gathered within these surveys is available in a 3D format with metadata to be integrated into digital workflows. If the surveys that follow are supplied as static 2D drawings without adequate descriptions attached to objects, they cannot be considered to meet BIM standards. The focus should, however, be on workflows. When procuring surveys, it is important to begin with the end in mind, with all information deliverables including surveys fit for the specific purposes for which they will be used. It is worth remembering that lean processes require that no extraneous information is delivered.

Geotechnical

A geotechnical survey will be needed when there are questions about the structure of the soil, or where significant movement of soil will take place as part of the project. This should provide detailed 3D information on the structure and strength of the site's geology.

Archaeology

While archaeological surveys are principally desk-based, site visits may be necessary, particularly on infrastructure or other large-scale projects where archaeologically significant findings are likely. There are a number of technological advancements that can integrate with BIM processes: ground penetrating radar, for example, can be used to populate a landscape information model with 3D information, allowing the design team to work with underlying or surface archaeology.

Arboriculture

The tree surveyor will note the species and health of trees on site, canopy spread and root protection area. A point cloud survey of the site can allow much of the work to be desk-based, but a site visit will be required to gauge tree health. BS 5837:2012 (BSI, 2012) sets out recommendations and best practice for the management of trees on site and provides a numbering system for creating tree records. This standard takes a paper-based approach to documentation; whether this is complied with strictly or a more technology-based approach taken is a matter for debate within the project team.

Ecology

The ecologist's Phase 1 habitat survey is the initial tool for assessing the ecology of an area, although further surveys may be required for species identification on a site. Ecologists often use GIS systems, meaning their surveys can be readily overlaid on the baseline survey and geographical context. The ecologist's work in a project's early stages influences when and where work should take place, to minimise the impact on protected species. Ecological surveys may continue long after the initial development as part of specific site requirements, and as such large bodies of data can be collected.

Soil survey

The landscape consultant will be focused on the capacity of soil as a growing medium, on water table and groundwater levels, and any contamination. Sampling boreholes should be identified as defined in BS 8574 (BSI, 2014a); professional judgement should be used to decide the required level of precision. Whether a soil scientist, geologist or landscape architect is responsible for the soil survey, the surveyor will use the employer's requirements to determine the information that should be passed into the model. The model will therefore contain various amounts of information defining the 3D extents and location of soil volumes of interest, such as contaminated soils or shallow growing media.

Underground asset survey

Underground services and assets on site should be surveyed according to PAS 128:2014 (BSI, 2014b), requiring an initial desktop survey, site reconnaissance, detection and verification. The objects that are developed should be specified to include any underground assets detected as well as any metadata describing them – for example, diameter, purpose (sewage, electrical etc.) – and should be provided in formats of use to colleagues who are part of the external works team. Technical surveys are important in reducing the risk of unforeseen cost or time expense. Information should be available to the whole project team via the CDE, and the data from these surveys added to the base survey data in the correct position.

References

BSI (2012) *BS 5837:2012 Trees in relation to design, demolition and construction. Recommendations.* London: British Standards Institution.

BSI (2014a) *BS 8574:2014 Code of practice for the management of geotechnical data for ground engineering projects.* London: British Standards Institution.

BSI (2014b) *PAS 128:2014 Specification for underground utility detection, verification and location.* London: British Standards Institution.

CHAPTER 14

Post-completion

Introduction

Once the project is handed over, the landscape management and operation phase begins. BIM Level 2 is ultimately about serving the needs of the users and managers of an asset, and it is in this phase that the success of these efforts can be judged. This chapter covers the resources available for ensuring the greatest benefit to those who will be using and managing the landscape, and the opportunity that this stage of the project life cycle offers for learning lessons. It should be noted that the savings requirement outlined by the 2011 Government Construction Strategy on built assets can be largely achieved post-completion, where the majority of costs arise (HM Government, 2011).

Some readers will have noticed that the construction period has not been covered. This is intentional. The requirements for site visits and snagging works are so significantly reduced during the BIM process, and so few requests for information or amendments to the design are likely, that it is possible to move on to a discussion of the post-completion phase without omitting any significant BIM details.

Starting with the end-user

BIM offers various tools to enable the creation of a functioning user-friendly landscape and to bring managers and users into the development process early on: the EIR, which provides a contractual obligation to meet the employer's requirements; PAS 1192-3:2014 (BSI, 2014), which sets out how the operational landscape's information is managed; and GSL (Government Soft Landings, 2013). A BIM Level 2 project begins with the end in mind, and these tools combine to ensure that the landscape handed over to its users and managers is fit for purpose.

BIM stresses the importance of learning lessons from projects and embedding them within future work streams to capture any innovative cost reduction or quality enhancement techniques for implementation on future projects, either by the employer or the project team. This has particular relevance when teams work together frequently, when long-term relationships are established with the employer, or when the employer develops very particular types of assets.

PAS 1192-3:2014

This standard is intended to ensure that information in the model for the design and construction of the landscape is transferred into its operational phase. It specifies that the information produced by the project team should be available in a single up-to-date version that correctly represents the development. Checking the model should therefore be all that is needed to see the assets that exist. It also offers improved facilities management processes, as problems and solutions can be readily identified by having the right information to hand.

This PAS enables asset, facilities and landscape managers to feed into the project initiation documents, specifically the Asset Information Requirements (AIR) and Organisational Information Requirements (OIR). These requirements might target specific benefits, such as:

- reduced costs resulting from the automated transfer of accurate, complete and unambiguous information at handover and during transfer of operations from one service provider to another
- greater awareness of the operational and maintenance needs of landscapes
- better decisions regarding operation and maintenance expenditure based on actual landscape performance and status
- earlier identification of poor performance and faults by gathering data from dynamic measuring and condition-sensing devices
- improved organisational and strategic planning from having complete and accurate landscape information
- higher information quality as a result of the automated verification introduced by the oversight requirements

Government Soft Landings (GSL)

BIM Level 2 requires that GSL is embedded within the project team's activities at every stage. It enables the design and construction team to provide a graduated extended handover to the landscape's users and managers, and helps the employer hold on to the 'golden thread' of the asset's intended purpose, with an assurance that the plans being implemented meet the original aims. An employer will include a soft landings strategy within the EIR, and consideration of the commissioning and maintenance aspects of a BIM Level 2 project begin during design. This benefits landscape-related industries in many ways. For instance, problematic aspects of designs can be identified before they are implemented, so that amendments can be made before construction begins, which can result not only in a better quality design, but also in one which is easier and less costly to maintain. Landscape features can also be changed in the design stages to meet the needs of users. While the GSL process is ongoing throughout the development of an asset, it is during the handover and post-completion period that it delivers its benefits.

GSL Champion

A GSL Champion is part of the project from inception, as an independent third party with no direct relationship to the project team or the employer. They facilitate the handover of the project team's work and carry out the post-occupancy evaluation against which the project as a whole, including the landscape, is judged, with the aim of ensuring that the social, environmental and economic requirements of the project are met. Post-occupation users have the opportunity to make their requirements known, and the relevant project team members will respond.

GSL has significant potential to improve the outcomes of designed landscape areas. A landscape delivered with GSL meets the employer's requirements and those of its users because the project team has responded to their input during design, and continues to do so after handover. It is a useful indicator for the employer in assessing how successful the project has been. As the impacts of a design may be realised years after construction, a longer and more involved care period gives landscape professionals more chance of avoiding shortfalls between design intent and realisation. The project can be managed more effectively and the design can respond to the needs of users when the requirements of those managers and users are understood. Furthermore, those maintaining a landscape will have prior understanding of what is required of them to enable the landscape to fulfil its purpose. GSL can raise the profile of landscape managers by including them in an intelligent, proactive and responsible handover and management process, and potentially the lesson-learning feedback loop of subsequent projects.

The knowledge within the GSL team can enable a better understanding of changes that might be needed in the design, construction and operation of the landscape, and of the opportunities and risks. The following activities all work towards a soft landing.

Inception and briefing

By increasing employer and user involvement within the project in early phases, many of the problems that only become apparent later in the project life cycle can be avoided. Performance criteria for the landscape should be established early on, in order to manage the handover of the landscape and its operational costs. As the project develops through the stages, the project team will have these targets to work towards, and the employer's team can develop plain language questions specific to these requirements. This also allows greater clarity in prioritising requirements for particular targets, so rather than focusing on a specific BREEAM score alone, for example, the employer can be part of the discussion to ensure that the BREEAM points that they meet are closely aligned to their objectives for the project.

Design development and review

GSL reviews can help to check that the team is designing ideas that will work, and that users will get the most from the assets. The specialisms represented at GSL meetings ensure that resources are well managed so that the end product can be used and maintained more cost effectively.

Pit stops

Project 'pit stops' take place under GSL, whereby the employer's team, GSL Champion and project team meet together to review work and revise as appropriate. The meetings are intended to be a collaborative environment for the open and honest sharing of information and discussion of issues, and are conducted in plain language to ensure that professionals' technical input is communicated clearly and understood. Representatives of key stakeholders from the employer's, design and construction teams should be present. At each meeting the issue under discussion is agreed beforehand, phrased simply in the terms of the plain language questions that are part of the EIR, and the meeting is kept specific to an agreed particular topic.

Pre-handover

The operating managers' understanding of a landscape's design intent is critical to its success. Ensuring that technical information is available to those who need to understand the performance of a landscape, as well as providing information to users and managers, helps these groups to appreciate the potential of the landscape and their role. This is particularly the case when the design involves ideas or strategies that are not necessarily obvious, which also requires a more intensive and prolonged dialogue between all parties.

Initial aftercare

The period immediately after handover is the time to roll out training to users and managers of landscapes. Training should be set up in advance to ensure that the correct information is given, and to plan resource allocation appropriately to avoid waste. Meeting with users and maintainers of the landscape and sharing information about its use and maintenance helps the design team to accommodate their needs and adapt the landscape as needed. The usual snagging processes still take place, but with a greater input into the maintenance practices anticipated by the design and construction teams. Inspections, meetings and site visits provide the opportunity to discuss how information is shared and agree any changes to this process that may be required.

   This approach requires a no-blame culture in order to work effectively. Issues that are discovered as part of the initial aftercare process should be treated as lessons to be learnt. The employer is buying into a long-term view of cost reduction, and should be mindful that outlays associated with extra training and other activities promoting optimum use of the landscape are part of an investment process that ultimately reduces operational costs.

Extended aftercare and post-occupancy evaluation

As the landscape settles into regular use, a number of activities take place to ensure that it continues to meet the needs of its users. Logging, site visits and meetings with members of the GSL team can identify changes required to help the landscape function more effectively. The commitment to aftercare must be made early in the commissioning process for the project. As the majority of costs within a landscape's life cycle occur during operation, an extended aftercare period and post-completion changes can help minimise these costs and realise considerable savings.

The Asset Information Model (AIM)

The two principal tools for managing asset information post-handover are the same as those in the design and construction phase, namely the CDE and the information model, which in this phase is now known as the AIM. The only changes required are those that support the facilities, landscape and asset managers, and their software needs. Migration from one CDE service to another or relocation onto the asset operator's own server is common. If there are changes in software systems, these should be planned to ensure an efficient handover of information at this stage.

If the facilities management team has software that can read COBie, the COBie deliverable that has been developed up to this point can now become a useful tool for transferring information from one system to another. Once transferred, the information will need to be managed in a way that suits the needs of the operations managers. Above all, the information should be issued in the AIM in the form required by the EIR, which may specify a method of information delivery that suits the employer's IT systems and landscape management practices. GIS and time management packages are often used for storing information on landscape management, so the AIM will be only one part of the total information in use.

Maintenance activities are logged as part of the AIM to ensure that it remains up to date and provides an accurate description of the landscape. The landscape manager's activities are principally reactive and planned, or a combination of the two, and their information requirements reflect this. For instance, it may be decided that a meadow is mown at given intervals, but the specific dates of these activities vary depending on factors such as weather and ground conditions.

When an asset reaches the end of its useful life or a major overhaul is required, the information model will ideally form the basis of the next phase. The AIM will become the PIM again and the process of generating information deliverables will start afresh, although from a more informed standpoint; the AIM can be used to monitor the maturity and establishment of site vegetation during redevelopment, for instance. A landscape that is managed using PAS 1192-3 (BSI, 2014) through the Asset Information Requirements document can inform a project operating under PAS 1192-2 (BSI, 2013). These standards can then work hand in hand with the other BIM Level 2 standards to ensure the production of high-quality information to match the requirements of the landscape at any stage of its life cycle. At refurbishment or redevelopment the asset moves cyclically from Stage 7 (in use) on to Stage 0 (strategic definition), now a common life cycle in modern construction. In future, many BIM Level 2 projects will be accompanied by a wealth of useful information enabling the best use to be made of existing site features.

Learning lessons

Once a project is complete, the design and construction teams often go their separate ways and the innovations that enabled things to be done better within and between teams are lost. Learning lessons and applying them is key to achieving favourable post-occupancy evaluations in GSL; projects are assessed on performance, cost and lessons learnt for application in future projects. Monitoring planting loss and replacement rates, and maintenance data relating to the project's life-cycle cost, for example, may also provide valuable quantitative data.

The principle of learning lessons applies just as much to project team members developing their own team working and collaboration processes as it does to the business of design. Collaborative working involves a certain amount of mutual education, and with a system for review in place this learning can be used and built upon. Taking time during the operation of a project to capture and review improvements can enable project teams and members to learn and develop during the project and beyond.

References

BSI (2013) *PAS 1192-2:2013 Specification for information management for the capital/delivery phase of assets using Building Information Modelling.* London: British Standards Institution.

BSI (2014) *PAS 1192-3:2014 Specification for information management for the operational phase of landscapes using building information modelling.* London: British Standards Institution.

Government Soft Landings (2013) *Government Soft Landings micro-site.* London: Department for Business, Innovation and Skills. www.bimtaskgroup.org/gsl

HM Government (2011) *Government Construction Strategy.* London: Cabinet Office.

CHAPTER 15

Landscape management and maintenance

Introduction

Soft works, hard works, furniture and other objects all require ongoing monitoring and maintenance, and performance of these tasks requires robust information about the site and what exists within it. This is currently provided by the asset list or schedule and the management plan, but as static documents they cannot be interrogated by software. Whether an object is a tree or an area of paving, recording is required not only for effective management, but also to enable the interpretation and analysis of data. BIM offers the landscape manager richer information about a site in this regard, creating scope for improved management. BIM emphasises the need for clarity of detail and predicted requirements for the planned management and maintenance of 'stable elements' or fixed assets.

An effective landscape management strategy will allow for the seasonal variations and unpredicted events that are a part of the life cycle of any landscape. BIM has the potential to create comprehensive site records, which over time could significantly improve maintenance. This chapter looks at the management of landscape assets electronically, in particular working with GIS and BIM, and the production of an AIM that meets the needs of the landscape manager.

Designing for site conditions

An understanding of how the landscape will change over time in order to design for site conditions is intrinsic to landscape professional practice. This is achieved by integrating design intent with management and maintenance practices; the tools and expertise of those maintaining a landscape are the greatest influence on how a landscape looks and functions from day to day, and how it evolves in the long term. A combination of design, maintenance skills and tools is essential; the right tools and skills are needed to manage the design, and the design should accommodate the tools and skills available. Apart from maintaining the landscape's aesthetic and ecological value, management of the health and safety of maintenance operatives on site is essential, requiring dialogue between the landscape architect and landscape manager, facilitated by GSL, to ensure a smooth handover of a landscape that is safe to use. Features of a site that pose safety issues during the operational phase should be designed out, or their danger mitigated at the earliest opportunity.

Reactive and planned maintenance

Landscape maintenance activities are either reactive, or planned to meet performance criteria. Planned maintenance tasks occur within a given time period, with a certain amount of leeway. Reactive tasks require the manager to monitor events and respond with appropriate maintenance; for example, a damaged play item will require replacement, preferably with a similar or identical item to avoid the need for redesign of the surrounding safe fall area. BIM supports maintenance activities by enabling time and cost calculations for specific tasks, for instance, and access to model and manufacturer information on equipment and supplies. The ability to plan the movements of team members carrying out works and the logical next best movement is important; the scope for reducing waste and generating greater economies increases significantly as the number and variety of tasks rises.

Managing landscape electronically

The electronic management of landscape assets happens at two distinct scales: the site-specific and the multi-site. Working within a single site, the manager will maintain information about the objects on site, their location and status, and any hazards. At larger scales the same information will be stored, but the complexity is increased with additional information on the teams responsible for each site and their different regimes, for example.

There is a wide variety of software options, depending on the size and quantity of the landscapes and objects being managed, and the resources available to employers and landscape managers. The software basis for managing the landscape should be kept in mind in preparing the AIM. Its ease of use for managers and operatives is key to ensuring that the design intent is effectively communicated, that the status of assets and other objects is correctly recorded, and that there is always a clear picture of the status of the landscape. Equally important is the ability of those managing the landscape to maintain it as it adapts and evolves as part of a lessons-learnt approach.

At the site scale, spatial information such as drawings and models remain largely unused in digital format. At the larger scale, asset information is stored on a GIS and thus has a strong relationship with the asset's location. Data-rich models can be provided at both scales, by various techniques. At one end of the spectrum is a single tool with an associated database; at the other end, BIM, GIS and other tools can be brought together using a spatial or relational database to connect software packages and the information they contain. The information created should be storable and viewable on a variety of platforms.

GIS and BIM

A closer relationship with BIM is a natural fit for existing management processes in a number of areas; in others, more work is needed to generate and manage the information. An assessment should be undertaken of the costs and benefits of integrating a landscape management system with a BIM workflow. BIM clearly integrates effectively with management systems that already use GIS or BIM tools to manage information and spatial arrangement. It makes sense to integrate assets such as statutory authorities' tree registers with BIM, for example, even if most processing tasks remain within the existing GIS workflow.

This interoperability is achieved by developing an information exchange strategy from the outset, or within the employer's strategic asset management plan. GIS and BIM data are structured within databases with a spatial aspect; with an appropriate geospatial coordinate system, an information model can be integrated into a GIS and vice versa. As a matter of course, tools that are intended for site-based design are the most appropriate for storing site data, while tools for larger-scale spatial data storage are appropriate for information about a wider area.

When planning the interface between GIS and BIM, the employer and their project team should consider responsiveness of the integrated data against accessibility. Where accessibility is key, a GIS with all the BIM data loaded into it for multiple sites will require significant computing power, but provides insights into the data held in these multiple files. Access to these models in one place can facilitate work planning, procurement strategies for future works and maintenance, as well as cost management.

If responsiveness is a priority, however, the GIS can provide links to open the BIM data in external packages instead of attempting to embed it; dedicated BIM tools will consistently operate better than a GIS package with BIM data. To strike a balance between accessibility and responsiveness, the AIM can be provided in a simplified graphical form with only the information deemed relevant by the asset and landscape management teams included. In every instance of a BIM–GIS interface, testing will be needed to ensure that the system operates as required.

Protocols will be needed for the future procurement of works in order for project teams to supply information that is interoperable with the system when the time comes. For a meaningful connection to take place, managers must be able to access information and search by location or type of object, for example. The information must also be editable, so that it can be kept up to date, with appropriate access controls so that only those authorised to make changes to assets can do so. Finally the information must be accessible to other software packages, so that if new issues arise or new management workflows are developed, the information underlying the system can be changed.

Classification systems

Classification systems and standardised information formats can help managers to plan effectively. Classification systems give an overview of activities, plans and the status of the landscape, using categorisation to group events within the landscape together to provide a greater understanding of the time and cost involved in maintaining the landscape than a list of individual occurrences offers. Systems in use within landscape include Uniclass 2015 and NRM 3, providing tools to plan cost management and procurement and allowing the manager to identify patterns and respond to them accordingly, either as programmed replacement or change during maintenance. For example, insight on replacement tree planting can be gained by viewing such events together. If a greater amount of tree planting is required than expected, the underlying reasons can be investigated and remedied.

The use and effectiveness of classification systems and management in general has been limited in the past by the quality of the information available. Prior to BIM, the requirement was generally for a quantity surveyor to aggregate and interpret information during the project stages, and the Landscape Manager thereafter. BIM now allows each professional to provide useful information to enable the calculation, management and forecasting of costs and design considerations.

Product Data Templates (PDTs)

PDTs are key to providing greater access to object information as a resource for the construction industry, via freely available data in a standard format. They allow manufacturers and suppliers to provide consistent product data that can feed into a BIM workflow, so that managers can easily add digital catalogue information into their AIM. PDTs have been developed by a number of professional institutions to cover industry-specific product data; the Landscape Institute is leading on developing templates for landscape products, which are available for free download from the LI website. Significant progress has also been made towards the development of PDTs by the manufacturing associations responsible for standardisation and specification requirements of products manufactured and supplied in the UK. Part of a sample PDT is shown in the appendix.

PDTs create a format for product data that offers a machine-readable alternative to manufacturers' information supplied in their own layout style or in non-computer readable form such as brochures. When considering the many material and object choices on a project, the spreadsheet or database that contains product information can be easily updated, and comparisons made between products on a wide range of criteria. Each individual object is entered into a Product Data Sheet (PDS) which is used on the project. The standardised format enables products to be swapped in and out easily, with all the product criteria automatically updating. So changing one paving unit for another, for instance, could allow a comparison on sustainability criteria, which when aggregated with all the other sustainability information would show how the choice between the two different products fitted into the overall project. As a result of their standardised layout, PDSs also offer a simpler option for exporting information.

TECHNOLOGY

Introduction

Part III of this book discusses the technological aspects of BIM, focusing on the needs of those involved in implementing technological changes within a practice. These chapters look at the processes required to navigate the IT aspects of BIM implementation, focusing on the technological tools for working with BIM at an organisational and project level. Discussion of specific software packages is beyond the scope of this book, so this section covers principles and good practice rather than particular products.

BIM-ready software ranges from packages that can link design objects to specification information, to fully integrated model-linked databases with customisable rule-based design. Software packages used in BIM projects need to be able to deliver information models. The information element of these models serves as the 'golden thread' for every project stakeholder. The project team can work with models produced by other consultants, gaining a greater understanding of the development; landscape managers can receive up-to-date information about the project, making maintenance work more efficient and effective, and clients can develop a better knowledge of their built assets.

The following chapters cover the digital outputs of a BIM project in terms of files and models, the tools used to create them, and issues for consideration in information sharing. The final chapter looks at where BIM is heading in the future, identifying some emerging developments and new directions for landscape.

CHAPTER 16

Digital tools

Introduction

This chapter starts by looking at the distinguishing features of software suitable for use on a BIM project. BIM is not software, and there is no out-of-the box, one-size-fits all BIM software solution; however, some specific software functionality is required to meet BIM Level 2 standards. After looking at the technological requirements, some criteria for selecting software are discussed. Questions to ask and issues to consider are suggested, both within a practice and in discussions with software providers and resellers, aiming to help IT managers and decision-makers identify packages that meet their strategic and business needs, from BIM authoring and design to cost management. This decision-making process starts with a look at a practice's strategic objectives, the requirements of BIM, and the common ground between them.

What software is suitable for use in a BIM project?

Two fundamental principles determine whether software is suitable for use in a BIM project: object-based design and information exchange. BIM processes are based on these key software functionalities. Object-based design connects information describing an object with the geometry by which it is visually and spatially defined. Information exchange, or interoperability, is the capacity to work with and share information with other software packages, without any loss or change to the information.

Parametric functionality is also key to BIM processes, in which a change made to one aspect of an object is cascaded to every view of that object, allowing greater control over the form of objects and their associated information. There are many parametric software solutions, and many drafting packages allow the use of parameters. The questions to ask are 'Will changes automatically apply to every instance or type of object?' and 'If an object is changed, will the specification also be updated?' In other words, to what extent does the software link the representation of objects with the information that describes them?

Software used as part of a BIM process has some other specific characteristics. First, it is intelligent, in the sense of an interaction between an object and the data defining it – for instance, allowing the modelling of a tree's growth over time and its interdependence with other trees. Intelligent software can also set rules to be applied automatically on the implementation of a design, giving the designer a warning if constraints are broken during the design process.

A second key software characteristic is enabling simulation and the creation of 3D models; furthermore, the designer is able to work with objects with their own attributes to create virtual models. This combination of graphics and information is vital to producing a virtual asset that can be used throughout the project's life cycle. Simulation allows the modelling of some critical features, such as climate, heat and movement. It can enable rapid calculations and better-informed decision-making. Software used in BIM is moving towards virtual design that accurately represents a physical site, and 3D models are often envisaged as the ultimate BIM tool. Modelling objects with their own attributes means that when one type of object is changed, every instance of that object will also be changed accordingly. The quantity of data that can accompany objects means that the range of design and analysis functions available is constantly expanding, serving to deliver the principles and aspirations of BIM still further.

The underlying technology within software tools determines their effectiveness in a collaborative project environment. Database functionality requires that objects are classified in a database, which should be arranged semantically to allow queries to be run. Uniclass 2015 is the classification system required for BIM Level 2, but there are a number of other classification systems in use across the construction industry. Information management functionality should allow the syntactic and semantic association of objects and the interoperability in information exchanges between other packages and users, as well as internally.

'Uses of BIM' software capabilities

The 'uses of BIM' concept (Kreider and Messner, 2013) offers a helpful perspective on how software may be used in BIM projects, categorising operations by function under the headings of gather, generate, analyse, communicate and realise. This classification of aspects of a BIM-enabled workflow highlights the role of technology within the design of built environment projects; a package that creates a 3D model from a point cloud survey can be part of a BIM process as much as a digital tool for creating planting schemes, or performing cost calculations.

Gather

Gathering is the capture of information about a facility or landscape, which allows the measurement and identification of objects and enables the management of the BIM process. Software processes that can collate and interpret surveying data are one example of the gathering functionality. For example, a project team that has gathered information about a proposed development can do an early quantity take-off, enabling cost management processes to begin sooner.

Generate

Generating refers to placing specific elements into a design, from plotting general features such as topography to individual objects such as street furniture and planting (Figure 16.1). This process includes defining objects and their position, as well as specific details such as performance requirements. Objects are generated at a specific Level of Detail and for a specific phase of the project; for example, the placement of planting or hard works within the landscape.

Analyse

An exciting aspect of BIM analysis is the ability to predict an asset's performance in use, before construction actually begins. This can show how a design will be used or how it will work within its environment in many ways; for example, water flow as run-off and within piped runs, slope analysis, aspect analysis, hill shade analysis, Zones of Visual Influence, sun and shade analysis, rainwater collection volumes, parking capacity, crowd simulation or vehicle simulation. Understanding climatic factors and usage of the site in the design stages helps ensure that designs are fit for purpose, although it is important to remember that analysis offers likely scenarios not certainties. These types of analysis can help the employer's team and future users of the site to understand an asset's design better, and facilitates more useful feedback throughout the development process. Analysis can also show whether a design is proceeding correctly, and identify clashes within designs.

Figure 16.1 Design tools can generate conceptual models to illustrate the design intent

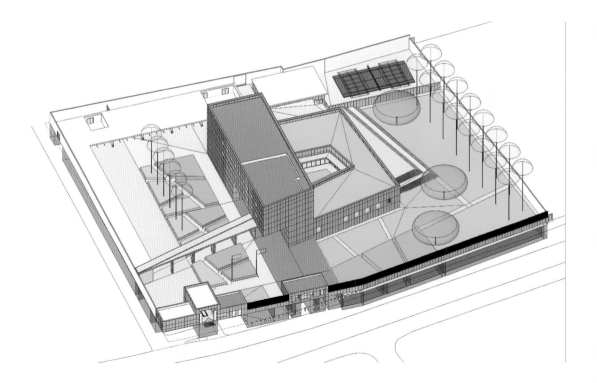

Communicate

The communication functionality of software in BIM projects means that every stakeholder in a project who needs information can access it. Information exchange is
fundamental to BIM and facilitates many of its other functions. For instance, generating visualisations, whether static, animated or interactive, provides a realistic
representation of the asset and enables the employer to assess or demonstrate its
intended use (Figure 16.2). Software can also generate images to display data visually.

Realise

Realisation refers to the physical creation of an asset and the various elements that
make up the whole. Software can provide the necessary information in the right
format to the correct standard to enable off-site fabrication or the on-site assembly
of design components or systems, for instance, as well as clash detection. It also
allows construction tasks to be streamlined, such as scheduling contractors' work
on site for the smoothest operation.

Software tools for landscape

These categories of BIM capability are applied in this section to software that is commonly used in landscape practice, along with some BIM-specific tools, identifying
functionalities required for landscape BIM projects.

Landscape architecture software

Landscape-specific software provides the landscape practitioner with the tools to
design planting schemes and hard works, including the specification of materials and

Figure 16.2
Visualisations based on
accurate information
allow a design to be
clearly communicated,
and enable informed
decision-making by
project stakeholders

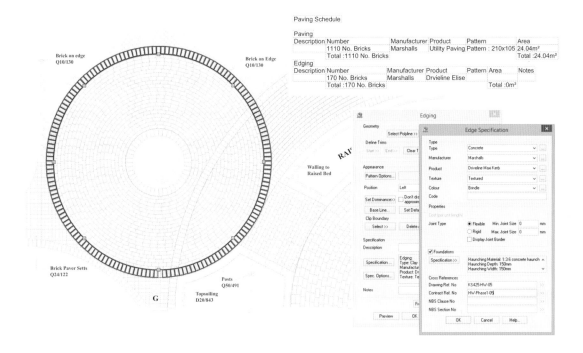

positioning of objects. The ability to apply simulations can demonstrate how plants and trees develop over time, for example, and 3D representations can demonstrate the design intent. The requirement to produce traditional 2D project documents within BIM Level 2 projects is met by these packages. Landscape tools also need to meet supply chain information requirements, including the capability to use manufacturers' or suppliers' information, as well as providing relevant information in a usable format for contractors and landscape managers (Figure 16.3).

Figure 16.3 Delivering information across the supply chain requires the clear identification of designed elements

Geographic Information Systems (GIS)

GIS is primarily an analysis tool, providing the facility to apply customised algorithms to multiple spatial datasets, which can be used for site context analysis, and as part of wider masterplanning and regional development strategies. It can be used at regional level to monitor the impact of development, or bring together a number of developments within an asset portfolio. At site scale GIS can monitor how the site is used and responds to its environment over time. This can provide insights into site performance and enable the identification of changes or enhancements to allow for different conditions on site, such as management of areas prone to flooding, for instance. Although traditionally a 2D package, GIS is increasingly able to incorporate 3D model information and combine geographic datasets with BIM information and imagery to enable visualisation.

Geodesign tools

Geodesign tools can generate masterplans at site and super-site scale to develop options and analyse them against a site's context. The ability to prescribe the size, materiality and location of proposed development types within a landscape context gives geodesign tools an extra dimension to GIS. For example, placing 3D realistic wind turbines in the landscape for the purposes of a Zone of Theoretical Visibility enables a more realistic representation of the visual impact of such a development. This capability is augmented by the ability to generate road, water and flora 3D objects from 2D mapping data and overlay these on 3D topography (Figure 16.4).

Specification software

Specification software works with authoring tools to provide information about the installation and management of objects. As various materials and techniques are proposed by designers and contractors, the specification can be used to check whether these materials meet requirements. The provision of relevant information in digital form to project managers and contractors for planning and managing workloads improves oversight of a project, and ensures that the latest standards are implemented. Specification software should be able to exchange information with other tools used in the BIM workflow, with the capability to input design information and apply classification to objects as required. It should also be able to communicate this classification

Figure 16.4
Masterplanning in 3D facilitates a design that is both useful to the design team and immediately legible to external stakeholders

information to facilitate cost and therefore the classification of specifications required. This information should then be communicable to other software packages such as asset and facilities management packages, databases and spreadsheets.

Cost management software

Various cost assessment tools can be used within the workflow to determine construction and maintenance costs, based on materials and site information. A system must be able to gather quantified information in automated form about the materials and objects on site, and classify them by space, zone and region according to the site designations specified within the project COBie. (COBie is the exchange mechanism that enables information to be delivered across the life cycle of the asset, explained in more detail in Chapter 18.) This can be used to assess the initial site development costs, and then handed over to the management team as part of the Asset Information Model (AIM) for ongoing site costs monitoring. The analysis capabilities within the cost assessment and simulation process can forecast site costs from an early stage. Cost management can be coordinated with the project management tools to provide cost prediction milestones to inform the employer's decision points and to monitor progress.

3D BIM authoring software

BIM authoring software should be able to gather and incorporate existing site information, including geometry, project-relevant material and asset information. Applying properties to BIM objects within the tools allows elements of the objects to be specified; for example, price information or embedded carbon. Classifying spaces by assigning them to named zones or regions in a design can allow quantity and cost to be allocated by sub-space, enabling improved cost and project management. The software should be able to produce the appropriate level of graphical and information detail for each specific stage of the project. It should be possible to position design objects in 3D or based on rules with respect to one another, with site elements prescribed, arranged and sized so as to meet the performance requirements.

Analysis should be possible within the software, or it should offer the option to share information with other packages to allow analysis for additional technical services provided by the project team. It should be able to determine whether a design meets requirements through assessment against performance criteria; for example, checking whether a footpath meets the correct slope requirements. Where relationships between objects are defined during design these too can be tested for compliance.

Making information available to other software packages is a key activity of a BIM authoring tool. It must be able to export and import geometry and information relating to the objects being designed, enabling the design team to work collaboratively with the rest of the project team. It should provide a realistic representation of the site to allow project stakeholders to engage with the design, with a clear indication of materials and the spaces created, as well as diagrammatic representations of objects within traditional design views such as sections, elevations and orthographic views. BIM Level 2 requires 2D outputs from files, so the software needs to be able to produce the drawn information. In terms of realisation, BIM-authored information should be usable as part of the Project Information Model (PIM) and Asset Information Model (AIM) to enable the construction of the asset components and their management, respectively.

BIM viewing and review software

BIM review and viewing software brings together models in a federated form to coordinate information and resolve spatial clashes. The ability to coordinate files from different professionals is key to its success as an analysis tool, validating designs in relation to one another within the same 3D environment and identifying issues for resolution.

COBie software

COBie provides for the maintenance requirements for specific objects, with the hosting software highlighting the appropriate management of scheduled tasks. It also provides a useful source of information on as-built assets so that managers can replace items correctly and easily when needed. By providing a standardised format for information, the COBie can enable the visualisation of analytics based on the whole site's performance. It can be used to control and regulate the construction process as it serves as the central repository for information on all planned works for maintainable assets.

COBie can be managed in different software packages; a spreadsheet is appropriate for COBie in table form, whereas a database should be used for XML. COBie can be exported from within BIM authoring tools or by altering other files to match the COBie structure. Assigned by space, zone and region, objects should be classified in terms of both their location and their association with a component, system or assembly, so they can be filtered and analysed within these terms.

The Common Data Environment (CDE)

All consultants should be working from the latest versions of files, so a common platform for version control should be established that meets the project's agreed standards. All project information is available on the CDE, a highly transparent project management tool where all activity on files is recorded, providing auditability and robust version control.

Clash detection

Also known as clash avoidance, this is the process of examining different project teams' models and identifying any overlaps or interfaces that require changes. When the virtual model is correct, the likelihood of discovering that designs need amendment or of costly mistakes being made in construction is greatly reduced – one of the major benefits of BIM.

A user can perform intra-software clash detection, importing another consultant's model into the same package with which it was created, and clash-detecting within that software. Extra-software clash detection can be used when working between different packages, using specific clash detection software. Manual clash detection is essentially the norm, however. While software can semi-automate the process, clashes still require identification and interpretation by an experienced professional inspecting the interfaces of their work with that of other consultants. Clash detection activities should be planned as part of the process of establishing the requirements of a BIM project at every stage.

Digital Plan of Works

BIM Level 2 requires the ability to manage information deliverables and their content, as well as responsibility for completing or feeding into them. The BIM Toolkit allows tasks to be allocated on a stage by stage basis according to the RIBA Plan of Works. Tasks may be assigned to one consultant within this process using any classification system for the numbering of tasks and Uniclass 2015 to choose the objects to be created. It also includes a Level of Detail option for every element that defaults to the LoD appropriate for the stage in which the task is assigned (Level of Detail is explained in full in Chapter 19). The Toolkit is intended to serve as a reference point for the tasks assigned rather than a project management tool, although it does include a number of features that enable the project team to make notes and comment on tasks and deliverables.

Reference

Kreider, R.G. and Messner, J.I. (2013) *The uses of BIM: Classifying and selecting BIM uses*. University Park, PA: Pennsylvania State University.

CHAPTER 17

Digital models

Introduction

Models simulate designs; each type, from the physical model to the multifaceted information model, has its own specific advantages that are suited to a specific purpose. Modelling requires the modeller to explore multiple dimensions of a design, from a 3D concept of an idea, through to usage of the scheme over time. Considering other types of model is helpful in appreciating that information modelling within BIM is just another form of modelling, with its own inherent requisites. The types of model looked at in this chapter are:

• the physical model
• the computer science model
• the Building Information Model
• the information model

The physical model

BIM modelling mirrors many of the functions of physical modelling. The purposes are alike: a physical model can show a development at different project stages with different levels of detail, and the modelling process helps in developing designs, exploring options and engaging with stakeholders, just as the digital model does. Like a physical model, a BIM begins as a simplified representation, but then starts to associate real-world information with the graphical, increasing in detail and complexity beyond anything a physical model could achieve. Material volumes, planting species and all the detailed non-graphical information that describes a project are connected with the graphical information in a continuing development of the design process until it becomes constructible.

The model of Buenos Aires in Figure 17.1 clearly shows the massing and relationship between grey and green infrastructure and between vertical and horizontal, as an aid to understanding proposals. A physical model requires no training to understand it; however, it is laborious to construct, the materials are not indicative of the final product and it is difficult to gather information about the design itself beyond the physical shape and the spaces created.

The computer science model

Figure 17.1 Physical modelling: Buenos Aires

Computer science theory underlies all the digital tools used by every professional within the built environment sector. Computers do not understand meaning, but they can classify through a shared ontology: that is, the naming and definition of the types, properties and relationships of objects. Where there is a shared ontology between software packages, both will recognise the properties of objects and define them with the same understanding. Humans understand that a hand forms part of an arm, which forms part of a human body, and more than that, these are all instances of body parts: also that the hand and arm have separate properties from the human and from one another. This must be explicitly defined for computers through a semantic understanding that relies not on where information about objects and assets is stored, but on being usable by other software programs.

The Building Information Model

BIM brings together the computer science and the physical models to work on the digital object, a Building Information Model (sometimes erroneously referred to as a BIM Model – think 'Building Information Model Model'). This model may consist of one or many files, containing information relating to every aspect of an asset. A digital object that can be visualised in 3D as a Building Information Model is different from other 2D or 3D models, thanks to its connection of geometry and information. Whatever else the software does or whatever other information the files contain, this is where the power of BIM tools lies. The connection of geometry with information creates far-reaching opportunities, not least in the process of model development, so that a change in a design updates all referring views and related objects to match.

This form of modelling means that complex data that describes a number of different objects can work together, providing a holistic understanding of a project at different levels of definition (Figure 17.2). BIM differs from other modelling techniques in its capacity to change the Level of Detail of geometry and information about objects, so that it is possible to move between a developed design and a massing model. In this way a BIM is not unlike a physical model, in that objects of varying complexity can be modelled elsewhere, and then swapped into the existing model to assess their fit with the design.

The information model

PAS 1192-2:2013 (BSI, 2013), the principal tool for achieving BIM Level 2 maturity on a project, does not use the term 'Building Information Model'; it refers only to an 'information model' and 'information modelling' with no building-specific connotations. An information model consists of documentation (as static read-only files), graphical information (all information that is presented visually), and non-graphical information, which covers the rest. The deliverables for a PAS 1192-2 interpretation of a BIM Level 2 project are native files, COBie and PDFs. The PDFs are the traditional deliverables on a built environment project: two-dimensional representations of the design in the form of sections, elevations and plan drawings. The COBie deliverable is the information exchange file that provides a consistent mechanism for sharing information about the asset and designed objects throughout its life cycle. Finally, the native file exchange enables the federation of models, bringing files together into one viewer or file for a combined view.

Figure 17.2 A Building Information Model is well suited to working with complex multidisciplinary designs

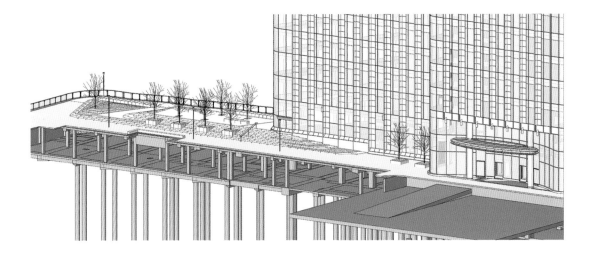

During the life cycle of a BIM Level 2 project, the contents of the information model evolve in line with the different development stages, and it goes through a number of name changes reflecting this. In the design and construction phase, the model is the PIM, the Project Information Model. It begins life as a design intent model, showing how the asset will meet the objectives of the employer, without including specific objects. When this model is resolved, with specific constructible elements in place, it becomes the Virtual Construction Model (VCM). The information required to bring the model to this standard is defined by the construction team responding to the project brief, the Employer's Information Requirements (EIR), and the conditions of the BIM Execution Plan (BEP). Once constructed, the model becomes the Asset Information Model (AIM), which is used by the management team in maintaining and running the asset.

The primary limitation to the capability of the BIM is the computer science model, which requires relationships to be created between objects and their parameters. The opportunities and constraints of the computer science model should therefore be considered in any BIM strategy. Intelligent objects can be created within BIM processes, but their relationships and the capabilities that underpin them are determined by the computer science model. So if a tree object is generated that can interact with the tree pit in which it is installed and can highlight surrounding structures at risk of root penetration, these relationships will have either been created specifically by the software developer, or by the user via the option to relate objects to one another within the software.

Reference

BSI (2013) *PAS 1192-2:2013 Specification for information management for the capital/delivery phase of assets using Building Information Modelling.* London: British Standards Institution.

CHAPTER 18

BIM files

Introduction

As mentioned in the last chapter, the file outputs required for BIM Level 2 are PDF, COBie and native file formats. Looking at the intention behind these outputs helps give an understanding of the information-sharing process. Although meeting these requirements is a consistent part of the narrative for BIM Level 2 projects, any BIM preparation process requires an understanding of these deliverables, along with a review of previous experience and lessons learnt, and input from the project team to identify what works best. This chapter looks at these outputs and discusses COBie in more detail, before looking at the options offered by the IFC exchange format and BIM data sources.

PDFs

The PDF is a common and open exchange format that can contain any kind of graphic content; PDF readers are freely available, and files can be created as read-only. This makes it a good medium for the traditional graphical requirements of a built environment design, namely 2D drawings of elevations, plans and sections. As a PDF can be marked up with comments or queries, it is an ideal replacement for the exchange of complete drawings on paper. However, copying a table from a PDF into a database or spreadsheet has wildly variable results, which makes it a poor format for information exchange.

COBie

COBie stands for Construction Operations Building information exchange. It is a subset of IFC, and offers a non-proprietary file format to facilitate the federated model concept. It is designed to list managed and maintained assets, ranging from the facility as a whole down to its fixtures and fittings, and to enable information to be delivered throughout the asset's life cycle. COBie can be represented as a data format, database or spreadsheet, but whichever is used, the data must correspond to a common standard and be exchangeable. COBie is intended to provide a mechanism for information exchange that should require little or no extra effort to gather information from multiple sources into a single store. Its use on BIM Level 2 projects is governed by BS 1192-4:2014 (BSI, 2014), which stipulates a UK-specific version of COBie that differs slightly from other versions.

COBie is intended to provide an accessible, clear and unambiguous overview of the total physical assets on site. This helps employer-side team members to define specific requirements for elements of the finished asset, and enables the project team to inform the employer of the assets delivered. However, given COBie's limitations in regard to landscape, the Information Manager should ensure that landscape information is included in another suitable form.

COBie structure

COBie is structured according to a hierarchy of objects shown in Figures 18.1 and 18.2. Each object is listed against a facility or asset. An object's position is defined first by a zone and a region outside the building envelope, then in granular detail within a space, where it is represented as a component. The object is further classified by type and the type of system of which it is a part. This means that a user can examine all objects within a given zone and region, objects of a specific type or those that form part of a specific system. COBie sheets should be auditable, with consistent codes used across the project, details of who has provided information and definitions of the information being provided.

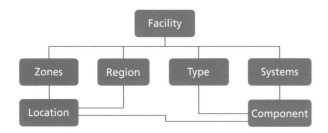

Figure 18.1 COBie hierarchy for infrastructure

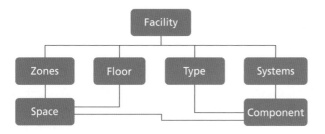

Figure 18.2 COBie hierarchy for buildings

COBie spreadsheet colour coding

COBie fields in spreadsheets are colour coded to describe their content, shown in Figure 18.3:

Required fields: yellow (RGB #FFFF00).
Fields that require the selection of a value from a list: salmon (RGB #FA8072).
Fields that might be completed by the generating software: purple (RGB #800080).
Fields required by the EIR or Digital Plan of Works (DPOW): green (RGB #008000).
User-defined fields: light blue (RGB #ADD8E6).

Required
Select option from list
Produced by software
Required by EIR or DPOW
User-defined

Figure 18.3 COBie spreadsheet colour coding

COBie sheets

The COBie as a spreadsheet includes the sheets shown in Figure 18.4.

IFC

The Industry Foundation Classes (IFC) platform was developed by and for the built environment sector to use to share information, and is considered the information exchange format most likely to become industry standard. As IFC was generated for buildings and is still developing, it is not yet a complete solution for geographical, civil engineering or landscape features (the Landscape Institute is involved in an initiative to include landscape assets within the next edition).

Fortunately the open file format specification means that software can be customised to produce and store information. Furthermore, a number of software packages allow the use of proxy objects, enabling users to define their own objects – which means that landscape professionals can create planting and other landscape-specific assets. A proxy object (referred to as an IFCBuildingElementProxy within the IFC schema) is an IFC entity such as IFCWall, IFCSlab or IFCFurniture, but with no specific object name attached to classify it. The external seat in Figure 18.5 is an example. The IFC has been adapted using the proxy elements of the object to enable the addition of information describing the bench, despite the absence of specific fields for the bench's attributes.

When imported into BIM authoring software as an IFCBuildingElementProxy object, the Product Data Template (PDT) information for an external seat classification can also be included, using the IFC Custom Property Set feature (see Figure 18.6). PDTs add a level of compatibility and transferability to the contents of files, so that those receiving these files know that the information was produced in accordance

Sheet Name	Purpose	Requirement
Instruction	Informs the user of the version of COBie used in the spreadsheet and may include guidance on use	
Contact	Details of an individual or organisation involved in the facility life cycle	Supplementary
Facility	A distinct asset, typically a site	
Region	A named intermediate spatial subdivision	
Zone	A named set of spaces sharing a specific attribute such as activity, access, management or conditioning	
Space	The location for activities such as use, inspection or maintenance: forms part of a region	
Type	Specification information related to components. Includes equipment, products and materials	
System	A set of components with a common function	
Component	Specific schedulable items and features that require management	
Job	Specific activity that occurs when the asset is being used	
Resource	Materials or skills required to complete jobs	
Spare	Replaceable parts of types	
Assembly	A combination of types and components that work together	Supplementary
Attribute	A characteristic of an asset	Supplementary
Connection	A connection between two components	Supplementary
Impact	Sustainability impact in economic and environmental terms	Supplementary
Document	The document associated with the asset	Supplementary
Coordinate	The spatial, GIS or other coordinates	Supplementary
Issue	Includes any risks or deficiencies associated with the assets	Supplementary
Supplementary information	Further information about the asset	Supplementary
Picklists	Where a picklist is specified for a field, the options available are specified within this sheet	Supplementary

Figure 18.4 COBie provides a highly auditable methodology for storing project information

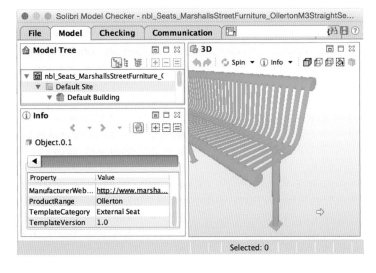

Figure 18.5 The IFC is capable, with some customisation, of describing any aspect of the built environment

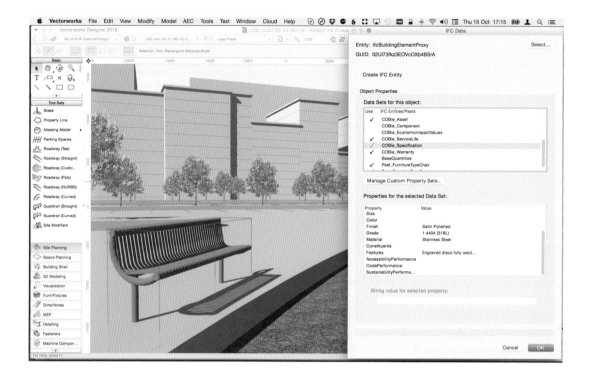

Figure 18.6
Information-rich models provide the same level of visual detail as other 3D models

with the current industry standard for landscape information. This demonstrates the flexibility of the IFC schema, as it allows any real-world object to be defined by geometry and data, and exchanged between software platforms. As an IFC proxy uses the same underlying structure as other object types, users have the same ability to edit geometry. Moreover, any property set or custom property set can be created, attached to the IFC proxy object, exported, imported, analysed and further edited in the receiving software.

Quality of information

The primary consideration in information exchanges on a BIM project is the intended use of the files. Some data will also be more useful than others. BIM Level 2 is about supplying value to an employer and reducing waste, while finding a balance between graphical precision, information and performance. The provision of too much information or performing unneeded work on a model means the employer obtains the same value from the project, but with more waste. It can also burden the project team; graphical over-precision can make a model difficult to render, for example.

Information should be clearly described before it is shared, as defined in the document control strategy for the project in the BEP. Suitability codes define the extent to which files can be relied upon, and the BEP indicates the software that should be used to open each file. It is important that ambiguity is eliminated in all forms of information exchange, and that the recipients and intended users of information should make preparations to use what they receive.

Software version

It is good practice to agree software versions at project initiation to avoid subsequent compatibility issues. It is advisable to work with the most recent version of a file format that all project team members can use, if possible. A software exchange protocol should be part of the project working methods to ensure that compatibility can be planned before project commencement, striking a balance between the functionality of the file format and its usability. In cases of uncertainty about compatibility, different methods may be required to ensure that file data is shared correctly.

Downloadable BIM files

Free downloadable content has been a feature of all digitally enabled industries since the earliest days of the internet, and the content of these files continues to be variable. If the provenance and quality of the data provided by manufacturers, suppliers and dedicated BIM object libraries can be verified, design teams can create a library of common objects and systems with time-saving benefits for designers. However, downloadable BIM files often have highly product-specific detail attached, which should be checked against the design and required Level of Detail defined within the Digital Plan of Works and BEP. Care should be taken that such objects conform to PDT standards to ensure that the parameters of similar objects can be easily and effectively compared. BIM Level 2 has presented manufacturers and suppliers with an opportunity to forge closer links with the design and construction sectors, and PDTs offer a common platform for the provision of product information – an interaction that forms part of a wider process of bringing all parties within the supply chain into greater engagement with BIM.

Reference

BSI (2014) *BS 1192-4:2014 Collaborative production of information Part 4: Fulfilling employers' information exchange requirements using COBie. Code of practice.* London: British Standards Institution.

CHAPTER 19

LoD

Introduction

LoD can stand for Level of Detail, Level of Definition or Level of Development, depending on context. It identifies how developed a design is, or how well defined the objects and spaces that make up a built asset are. The essential aspect of LoD is time; as the project progresses, the elements of a development change and designs and objects are refined. Put in its simplest terms, LoD initially indicates an object's existence; then, that the object has approximate dimensions, and must perform in a certain way, until finally detailing the specific object that is to be designed and then delivered.

Level of Development

Designed zones and objects are developed over time. A zone begins with an understanding of the overall brief that may indicate that there is, for example, a need for car parking. While the completed project is still far away in the future, it is known only that it will include a car park, the lowest level of detail. As the project progresses, the number of parking spaces comes to be known, and design then begins on the car park's objects, until eventually it is complete with kerbs, planting, and every other detail resolved and delivered.

In the UK under BIM Level 2, LoD stands for Level of Development, indicating the overall detail for an object or space. The Level of Development comprises two elements that describe the deliverable: the Level of Detail (also abbreviated to LoD), which represents graphical detail, and the Level of Information (LoI), which represents information detail. The Level of Development applied to a project defines information requirements for landscape objects, so that the project team delivers only the information required. A Level of Development is set for designed objects at each project stage, so that the project team is clear as to the requirements for information deliverables.

A model's Level of Development shows the extent to which the information within it can be relied on. For example, a highly defined model might describe the bolts to be used on a bespoke bench. If the Level of Detail indicates that this model can be relied on to show that there will be a bench in an approximate position and no more, the bolts can be disregarded as over-defined and subject to change as the design develops. Level of Development sits as a system of classification within the BIM Toolkit software. In conjunction with Uniclass 2015, LoD describes every possible deliverable on a built environment project. Very broad decisions can be made about an object at one stage, with more specific decisions coming later about the information attached and the visual appearance of the object. It is worth noting, however, that on larger projects other processes may exist for managing deliverables and the LoD within the BIM Toolkit may not necessarily be used.

Responsibility

Within the BIM Toolkit, an object is initially defined only by the team member responsible for the information deliverables. If aspects of a design require input from several project team members, these consultants and their specific responsibilities should be included – otherwise a landscape architect might, for example, find themselves

Level of Detail	Indicative graphical detail	Purpose
1	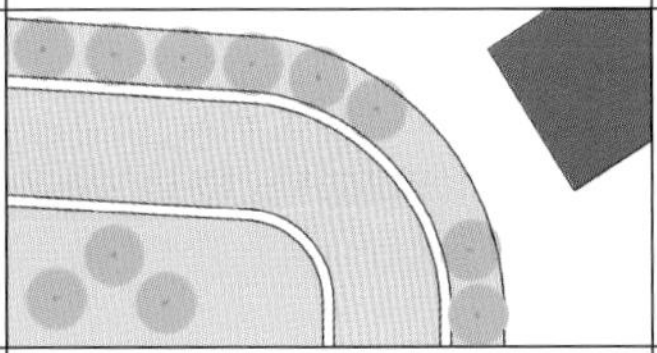	To provide a visual representation at the feasibility stage and assist the client to understand the project objectives and constraints.
2		To provide a visual representation at the concept stage that demonstrates the main principles of the design and how these may meet the client's brief.
3	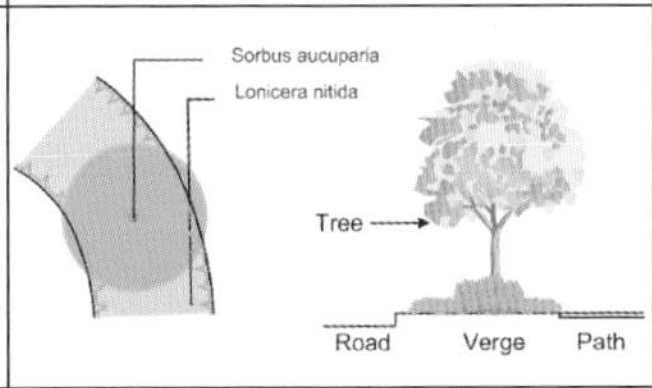	To provide a visual representation for design development that can be used to show the general arrangement and relationship between objects. Supports full spatial coordination.
4	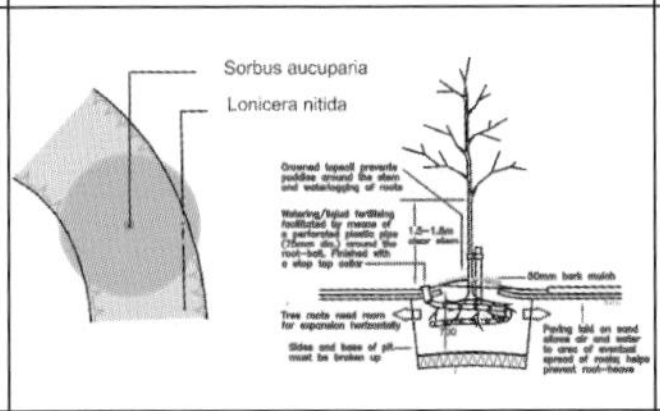	To provide a visual representation for technical design, sufficiently developed to progress procurement, project programming and construction.
5	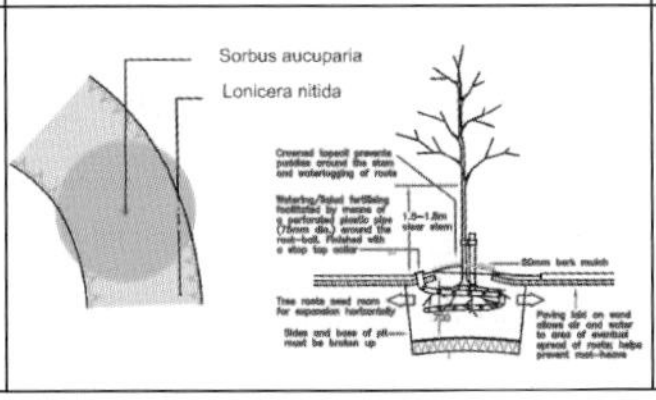	To provide a visual representation for coordination, construction and installation. The information should be updated to reflect the final design and support the operations and management of the asset.

Figure 19.1 Level of Detail

Figure 19.2 Level of Information

Level of Detail	Indicative graphical detail	Level of Information
2		To provide an outline description of the design intent and level of information required at the concept stage.
3	Tree → Road Verge Path	To provide relevant performance information about the object that can be used to assess purpose, function and maintenance.
4	Crowned topsoil prevents puddles around the stem and waterlogging of roots; Watering/liqid fertilising facilitated by means of a perforated plastic pipe (75mm dia.) around the root–ball. Finished with a stop tap collar; 1.5–1.8m clear stem; 50mm bark mulch; Tree roots need room for expansion horizontally; Sides and base of pit must be broken up; 700; Paving laid on sand allows air and water to area of eventual spread of roots; helps prevent root–heave	To provide sufficient technical design information regarding the assembly child products to allow suitable manufacturers to be considered. Information should cover completion and execution, such as preparatory works and construction requirements.
5	Crowned topsoil prevents puddles around the stem and waterlogging of roots; Watering/liqid fertilising facilitated by means of a perforated plastic pipe (75mm dia.) around the root–ball. Finished with a stop tap collar; 1.5–1.8m clear stem; 50mm bark mulch; Tree roots need room for expansion horizontally; Sides and base of pit must be broken up; 700; Paving laid on sand allows air and water to area of eventual spread of roots; helps prevent root–heave	To provide sufficient information in the construction phase regarding the assembly child products to allow purchasing, including manufacturer details, product reference and any specific options.
6	Prunus avium 'Plena' 175/200 cm Clr Stm 150-175 :5/7 brks Root Wrapped	To provide information for operations and maintenance regarding the installed deliverable, including the associated PDF manuals. The key properties will be transferred into an asset database.

responsible for the engineering requirements of a paved area. (In this case, the landscape architect should ensure that the engineering work for the paved area is complete and integrated into one deliverable before issue.) The responsibility for works will be allocated principally within the project contract; the landscape architect should not assume or find themselves responsible for any aspect of the project for which they are not competent. If the landscape architect is the design team leader, the co- or sub-consultants' responsibilities and roles should be made clear within the contract and within the BIM Toolkit.

Level of Definition in the BIM Toolkit

Within the BIM Toolkit, Level of Definition details the work required, and by whom and when it will be done. There are five Levels of Detail (Figure 19.1) and five Levels of Information (LoI) (Figure 19.2), which can be set to any level at any stage within a project. As the design process proceeds, an object's definition progresses through project stages from 1 to 7; these correspond loosely with the RIBA Plan of Works project stages, with a project life cycle that starts with strategic definition and ends with handover and close-out. The Level of Definition of objects is closely related to the stages in which they are conventionally specified. Objects will ordinarily be defined as having the same LoD and LoI as the stage number, unless the employer or a statutory authority requires unusual material use or object selection.

The value of Level of Definition lies in its potential to change information requirements on individual objects. This means that the project team knows how well defined objects should be at a given stage, and employers are able to define the information required for a particular stage of a project, in line with their needs.

CHAPTER 20

Interoperability

Introduction

Interoperability is the sharing of information between different software packages, with the potential to perform additional computations. At its most efficient, it is a rapid, automatic process invisible to the user, as for example when opening a text file in a word processor and finding the content exactly as it was produced by the originator, regardless of the software that created it. Designing, constructing and maintaining landscapes is a team-based process and, as such, information that supports decision-making should be readily available to each team member, for the smooth operation of the project as a whole. Effective interoperability creates a project environment where the benefits of BIM can flourish, where information is dynamically and easily shared between the project team and the employer so that important insights about the design of the project, its progress and its outcomes can be assessed at ever-earlier stages of the process. BIM currently requires a series of file formats to work together that were not designed with this in mind, however, so as sharing and exchanging information is key to BIM, interoperability is essential.

Syntactic and semantic exchanges

Information exchange can take place on two levels: syntactic and semantic. Syntactic interoperability means that one software package can use the same file format as another and that they can read one another's files. If one package produces a COBie as XML and another package can read that XML, that is syntactic interoperability. Syntax in this context refers to the arrangement and structure of information, such that a file format may be read and the content understood but not edited.

Semantic interoperability enables shared meaning within files. Using the previous example, once a COBie file has been transferred, semantic interoperability enables the receiving software to interpret, for instance, that the data within the contact sheet relate to a person or organisation and to treat them as such by bringing them into a contacts list. Understanding the difference between semantic and syntactic interoperability enables those who are planning and implementing BIM technology to gauge the success of information exchanges. When gathering information without a need for interpretation, syntactic interoperability will suffice. However, when more complex operations are required – for example, cost take-off or sustainability calculations – then information exchanges will need a level of semantic interoperability.

Information exchange mechanisms

Information can be shared between software packages by direct integration or file exchange. Direct integration occurs through an API (Application Programming Interface), which enables two software packages to communicate with each other in real time. So, for example, if a 3D modelling package has a microclimate analysis tool loaded through its API, it can now perform a new analysis function, and likewise the analysis software can work with the 3D model. These integrations may already be set up and just require the installation of a plug-in.

File exchange is the traditional method for information exchange. Files are saved in one of two categories: native or exchange format. Native files contain all the information required by a software package to generate the information that enables the core functionality of that software, be it design or analysis, structured in the correct way within their software. No two native file types are alike and they are all unique to the software in which they were created. Exchange format file types are designed for information sharing. As such they cannot enable the full functionality of every software package that saves within that format; what is exchanged is that which is common to a number of different software packages.

Interoperability strategy

An interoperability strategy enables information to be shared between software packages and file formats. There are common steps to follow, regardless of software or format, to achieve effective information exchange, and these should be documented as part of the workflow management of a project. The strategy should start with a statement of intent describing the need for the information exchange in plain language, identifying the software involved and the information to be passed between them. After that the stages are:

- plan
- prepare
- act
- learn lessons

This is a cyclical process that may require multiple iterations until the software's capabilities are understood and the required outputs achieved.

Plan

First, assess how the information exchange will take place and its expected benefit. This can be set out as a simple risk matrix (see Figure 20.1). How complex is the information exchange? Common exchanges that are performed frequently with minimal error can be said to be of low complexity, for instance. Second, what is the

Issuing software	Receiving software	Complexity of exchange	Value of exchange	Exchange viability
Software A	Software B	Low	High	High
Software C	Software A	Medium	Medium	Medium
Software B	Software A	High	Low	Low

Figure 20.1 Information exchange planning matrix

value of success? For example, a low value of success exchange might mean that an image needs a slight colour correction after exchange, whereas a high value of success exchange might require passing accurate component dimensions to a contractor to ensure a correct build process.

A plan for information exchange should specify the process to be followed; the following steps are suggested.

Exchange content and utility

The statement of intent will determine the content of the exchange; its use will determine the method of exchange.

Syntactic or semantic

Will the information be exchanged syntactically (loaded only) or semantically (also understood)? If information is needed only for recording purposes, a syntactic exchange will suffice; if further calculations are required, a semantic exchange is needed.

Federation or integration

Federation is required if the ownership and integrity of the source file must be retained, essentially making it uneditable upon loading. If the information is to be edited, integration is required. Federation ensures that liability remains with the file's originator, whereas integration and subsequent changes to the content may need to be recorded to manage liability.

Direction

Will information be passed one way only, or processed and returned? And will it then require further processing? One-way information exchanges that need no further processing should take little time; two-way exchanges that require processing at both ends will take longer to complete. The need for further processing should be minimised as much as possible; for instance, by installing software updates, or programming with the software's API to update its functionality.

Exchange mechanism

Will a file be used to share information, or will direct interaction be involved? The benefits of each approach should be considered in the light of software-specific knowledge resources and the experience available in the team.

Prepare

The right tools should be in place for the exchange. Direct integration requires the appropriate versions of each software package and integration plug-ins: file exchange may also require this. Specific preparation requirements may include the removal or simplification of unsupported information; for example, a software package may produce a unique terrain surface, which might need to be converted to a surface or volume compatible with the recipient software.

Units

Spatial position within the real world is of considerable significance to external designers. Programs that use the same units of measurement are unlikely to have problems exchanging this information, but exchanging between imperial and metric units, or millimetres and metres, will require further steps, such as scaling and reorientation.

Spatial arrangement

Three additional elements are required for effective coordination: the coordinates system, the base point for the project and the position relative to north. Coordinates systems can be classed as arbitrary or geographical; the use of the more complex geographic coordinate system (GCS) is recommended in any event, in order to work effectively with assets in a landscape context. When the spatial arrangement of a design is assured, the result is a model that is fit for purpose and can be exchanged readily with other members of the project team, which in turn means more efficient collaboration between consultants.

Act

A range of tests should compare exchange outputs with expected results, increasing in complexity until a full model is used. Testing should continue until it is certain that the exchange has worked correctly in high success priority information exchanges. Where the priority for success is lower, simpler tests may be used or the information exchange may be attempted first time.

Learning lessons

The results of the information exchange should be assessed against two criteria: relational integrity and completeness. Relational integrity means that after exchange, spatial information still describes the same points in space and non-graphical information still describes the same objects. A highly complete exchange transfers all the information in the manner expected. An information exchange that is both complete and retains its relational integrity can be deemed a success. Incomplete exchanges should be seen as part of the learning process; successful techniques should go on to become embedded within the practice's processes.

Exchange formats

A number of file formats can be used for information exchange.

IFC

IFC4 is an open standard created by buildingSMART International with the support of built environment professionals around the world for the purposes of 3D model information exchange. As an interim measure, landscape objects can be stored within the format as proxy objects, as seen in Chapter 18. This information should conform to the appropriate PDT associated with the object type or another suitable standardised classification system if no PDT exists.

XML

Extensible Markup Language (XML) has much in common with HTML, used to make websites. It is highly adaptable and a number of subsets have been built upon its format. It can contain any number of data structures and information sets, and is therefore particularly suited to information exchange purposes.

GML

Geography Markup Language (GML), based on the XML schema, was developed by the Open Geospatial Consortium as a geographical information exchange mechanism. It can store information about geographic coordinate systems (GCS), time, features and other geometry. As a generic format, it requires some additional work by users wishing to adapt it to add their own attributes.

CityGML

CityGML is an exchange format for information used to describe cities, based on GML. It can store information about land use, buildings, bridges, street furniture, vegetation, topography, tunnels, water bodies and transportation infrastructure.

LandXML

LandXML is designed to exchange civil engineering and geomatic survey information. It can share surfaces, point objects, roads, ponds and pipe work, and be used to exchange transport infrastructure, topographical and material information, and hydrological and survey data.

COBie

COBie is the designated exchange mechanism in the UK for non-graphical information relating to maintainable assets. It can be stored as an XML format and semantically integrated into software packages, enabling a greater usability of the information. In software that does not support IFC, COBie can be shared syntactically as a spreadsheet, which may require further steps to enable automatic and semantic processing.

BCF

The Open BIM Collaboration Format is another buildingSMART standard. It includes an XML file format and a Representation State Transfer (REST) web service, which means that programs can interrogate it easily and receive semantic information about the model.

.dxf

This open CAD file format is capable of exchanging vector geometry and text, but is no longer updated.

Shapefile (.shp)

This is an open standard GIS format that stores geometry and associated information with reference to a GCS. As an open format it has been adopted by a number of different software providers.

CHAPTER 21

The future

BIM Level 3 strategy

BIM is inherently forward-looking. The early BIM core maturity models defined progress as movement towards the goal of Level 3 BIM. Although initially an aspirational device, this goal has since been embodied in the government's Digital Built Britain Level 3 BIM Strategic Plan (Department for Business, Innovation and Skills, 2015), setting out the case for further government funding of BIM development. As part of the wider UK construction strategy, the BIM Level 3 vision has clear links with other government strategies for construction, business and professional services, smart cities, and the information economy. This will bring the built environment sector to work in concert with other sectors of the national economy to deliver innovation and growth. The goals of the Level 3 strategy are:

- to work towards an open data standard to facilitate data sharing across the entire market
- to establish a new contractual framework for projects that cements BIM
- to create a cultural environment that is cooperative, continually learning and sharing
- to train public sector clients to understand and implement BIM
- to drive growth within the UK technology and built environment sectors

The technical expertise within UK BIM is seen as the principal mechanism for achieving these outcomes, by driving innovations in processes and technologies to generate new techniques, as well as developing the BIM Level 2 model. This will be underpinned by a research-focused approach that works at cross-industry and international level to support these innovations with funding opportunities. Digital Built Britain will also use international support and funding resources across Europe, the Far East and Australasia. The future of Digital Built Britain is not a certainty, however. As BIM implementation develops, the industry will need to observe successes and lessons learnt in order to navigate to a project environment where the possibilities of Digital Built Britain can be realised.

The Level 3 model

It is envisaged that at Level 3 a single environment will contain all the information that defines a model. New software and techniques are constantly being developed, but the completely integrated single model has some way to go before becoming a reality. The BIM as a common platform for the entire development project was propelled into the imagination of the built environment sector in the UK by the Bew–Richards BIM maturity wedge, introduced in Chapter 2. The original definition of Level 3 maturity is: 'A fully integrated and collaborative process enabled by "web services" and compliant with emerging IFC standards. This level of BIM will utilise 4D construction sequencing, 5D costing information and 6D project life cycle management information' (BIM Task Group, 2011).

This and earlier definitions have led to confusion as to what BIM actually is. The core principle is: 'A fully integrated and collaborative process enabled by "web services" and compliant with emerging IFC standards.' This depends not only on the operations that software can perform on a combination of geometry and information, but also how well information can be passed into other software packages – in a word, interoperability. The powerful technology of BIM can sometimes be at odds with the lean construction aims. The creation of ever-richer information can mean rising costs and more time investment, and when this goes beyond what the client deems to be of value, it is no longer lean practice and is therefore wasteful.

Internationalisation

BIM Level 2 and its associated standards and specifications have delivered a unique approach to the implementation of BIM on built environment projects. The next stage for these standards is to become internationalised. Other countries such as Norway, Australia and Singapore have been pursuing their own implementation of BIM, and are also looking to create an international BIM standard. At the time of writing, this is under development, but the possibility of the UK standards becoming international is real, in the form of the developing international BIM standard, the ISO 19650 series – set to include the requirements of both PAS 1192-2 and BS 1192:2007. This would present a huge advantage for UK practices who have engaged with the BIM process, and give a further competitive edge over those who have yet to begin their BIM Level 2 journey.

Smart cities

The necessity for cities to respond more effectively to the needs of their inhabitants has never been more urgent. 'Smart cities' look for better operation and management of urban environments through smart technologies, often known as the 'internet of things'. Devices monitoring the use of resources are connected online to enable information to be fed back to those managing these assets, and to allow better and quicker decision-making, responding to rapidly changing circumstances. The drive to improve the management of technological and natural resources, from transport to water, has clear linkages with BIM's lean ethos and methods. In the

coming years, the UK government will be examining ways to expand its implementation of smart technology within the public realm, with the potential to create an
environment that is more responsive to the public's needs.

The potential for landscape

Landscape architecture provides a holistic approach to the planning, design and
development of built environment projects. The landscape profession has a significant opportunity to develop new landscape-led natural and social resources within
these emerging trends, leveraging BIM processes and technology. Engaging with
BIM means that more projects can benefit from the expertise of not just landscape
professionals, but also ecologists, arboriculturists and engineers who work outside
the building, who can reduce waste and add value to a project from the outset.

The walls of the construction sector's silo-based mentality are beginning to crum-
ble, and with a concerted effort, the development and implementation of BIM's
new tools and approaches promises to deliver more cost-effective projects, delivered
on time and within budget. This does not come without effort; every professional
wishing to operate in a BIM environment has to adopt a collaborative approach to
working, seeking methods of avoiding blame, and taking collective responsibility
for the efforts of the project team. Only a cohesive, collaborative sector can hope to
overcome the problems of the past. This attitude comes more easily to those who
are adapting to a work environment where knowledge is shared, information is used
to the full, and nothing is hidden; these are the professionals who will deliver the
promises of BIM.

References

BIM Task Group (2011) *A report for the Government Construction Client Group
   Building Information Modelling (BIM) Working Party: Strategy paper.* London:
   Department of Business, Innovation and Skills.
Department of Business, Innovation and Skills (2015) *Digital Built Britain: Level 3
   Building Information Modelling – Strategic plan.* London: Department of Business,
   Innovation and Skills.

Sample product data template

Template Category	**Flora**			
Template Version	**v.6.0**			
Category Description	**Plant species grown for the purpose of planting out in a landscape.**			
Classification System				
Classification	**Value**			
Suitability for Use				
Template Custodian				
Information Category	**Parameter Name**	**Value**	**Units**	**Notes**
Manufacturer Data				
Specifications	Manufacturer		Text	
Specifications	Manufacturer Website		URL	
Specifications	Product Range		Text	
Specifications	Product Model Number (Code)		Text	
Specifications	CE Approval		Text	Yes, No or the four digit identification number of the notified body involved in the conformity assessment procedure.
Specifications	Product Literature Webpage		URL	
Specifications	Product Features		Text	
Naming Data				
Specifications	Product Code		Text	
Specifications	Botanical Name		Text	
Specifications	Alternative Botanical Name/s		Text	
Specifications	Common Name(s)		Text	
Specifications	Category/Class/Type		List	
Specifications	Sub-Category/Class/Type		List	

Nursery Stock Data (taken from BS 3639 and NPS)				
Specifications	Height		cm	Range of values or Minimum value
Specifications	Spread		cm	Range of values or Minimum value
Specifications	Girth		cm	Range of values or Minimum value
Specifications	Clear stem height		cm	Range of values or Minimum value
Specifications	Number of breaks/buds		Nr	
Specifications	Form specified		List	
Specifications	Age and condition		List	
Specifications	Root condition and protection		List	
Specifications	Cell/container size		List	
Specifications	Planting Medium		List	
Specifications	Fertiliser		List	
Specifications	Origin and provenance		Text	
Planting Requirements				
Specifications	Aspect/shading		List	
Specifications	Acid/Alkaline		Text	
Specifications	Moisture		List	
Specifications	UK hardiness		List	
Specifications	Soil type		List	
Planting Selection Data				
Specifications	Ultimate height		cm	
Specifications	Ultimate spread		cm	
Specifications	Years to ultimate height		years	
Specifications	Habit/form		List	In its natural form or as maintained
Specifications	Foliage texture		List	
Specifications	Foliage colour		List	
Specifications	Foliage colour Autumn		List	
Specifications	Foliage persistence		List	
Specifications	Foliage shape		List	
Specifications	Flower Type		List	
Specifications	Flower Colour		List	
Specifications	Flower Season		List	
Specifications	Winter colour		List	Yes/No?
Specifications	Feature		List	
Specifications	Season of interest		List	
Specifications	Edible/cropping		List	Yes/No?
Specifications	Suitability/use		List	Is the list complete?
Specifications	Scent		List	
Performance Data				
Specifications	Growth rate		List	
Specifications	Effective life		Years	
Specifications	USDA zone max		List	
Specifications	USDA zone min		List	
Specifications	Tolerance		List	
Specifications	Toxicity/thorns/spikes etc.		Text	
Specifications	Biodiversity		List	
Specifications	Climate		List	
Specifications	Native region		List	

Sustainability			
Sustainable Material BREEAM etc.	Embodied Carbon	kgCO$_2$	
Sustainable Material BREEAM etc.	Life Cycle Analysis	Number	BREEAM
Sustainable Material BREEAM etc.	Location of Manufacturer	GridRef	Northing, Easting
Sustainable Material BREEAM etc.	Green Guide for Specification	Text	A - E
Sustainable Material BREEAM etc.	Environmental Product Declaration	Text	3rd Party Verification
Sustainable Material BREEAM etc.	Responsible Sourcing of Materials	Text	Endorsing body
Sustainable Material ETL	URL to Energy Technology List	URL	Hyperlink to ETL webpage for product
Sustainable Material LEED v.4	Responsible Extraction of Materials	Text	TBA
Sustainable Material LEED v.4	Material Ingredient Reporting	Text	TBA
Operations & Maintenance			
Facilities/Asset Management	URL to O&M Manual	Text	Hyperlink to Manufacturer O&M Data
Facilities/Asset Management	Daily	Text	Maintenance tasks or SFG2012 codes.
Facilities/Asset Management	Weekly	Text	Maintenance tasks or SFG2012 codes.
Facilities/Asset Management	Monthly	Text	Maintenance tasks or SFG2012 codes.
Facilities/Asset Management	Quarterly	Text	Maintenance tasks or SFG2012 codes.
Facilities/Asset Management	6 Monthly	Text	Maintenance tasks or SFG2012 codes.
Facilities/Asset Management	Annually	Text	Maintenance tasks or SFG2012 codes.
Facilities/Asset Management	Bespoke Timeframe	Text	Maintenance tasks or SFG2012 codes.
Facilities/Asset Management	Maintenance Required: 0–300hrs	Text	Maintenance tasks required during this time frame.
Facilities/Asset Management	Maintenance Required: 301–600hrs	Text	Maintenance tasks required during this time frame.
Facilities/Asset Management	Maintenance Required: 601–1000hrs	Text	Maintenance tasks required during this time frame.
Facilities/Asset Management	Maintenance Required: 1001–2000hrs	Text	Maintenance tasks required during this time frame.
Facilities/Asset Management	Maintenance Required: 2001–4000hrs	Text	Maintenance tasks required during this time frame.
Facilities/Asset Management	Maintenance Required: 4001–8000hrs	Text	Maintenance tasks required during this time frame.
Facilities/Asset Management	Maintance Required: 8001–12000hrs	Text	Maintenance tasks required during this time frame.
Facilities/Asset Management	Expected Life	Years	
Facilities/Asset Management	Warranty ID	Text	

Glossary

AIM/Asset Information Model   The information model that describes the asset as completed.

AIP/Asset Information Plan   The plan for integrating the Project Information Model into the Asset Information Model in response to the Asset Information Requirements.

AIR/Asset Information Requirements   The AIR is developed from the Organisational Information Requirements and feeds into the Employer's Information Requirements. It specifies the requirements for information delivered into the Asset Information Model from the Project Information Model based upon the operational requirements of those using and managing the asset.

Asset   The end result of a construction project, which may include landscape features.

BEP/BIM Execution Plan   A plan drafted and used by the project team to define how they will carry out the technological and process aspects of BIM on a project. The BEP sets out how the needs of the EIR will be met, and must respond in full to these requirements.

BIM Author   Also known as an information originator, responsible for developing the information model and producing the project deliverables.

BIM Champion   The person responsible for driving the implementation of BIM within an organisation. They may be appointed or self-appointed.

BIM Coordinator   An industry term for an operational BIM role responsible for administering the information management policies of an organisation or on a specific project. There is as yet no unified definition for the BIM Coordinator role and the specific responsibilities of different roles may vary.

BIM Implementation Plan   An organisational plan that is used to develop and review BIM implementation progress.

BIM Manager   An industry term for a BIM management role responsible for managing the BIM standards and implementing them on specific projects. There is as yet no unified definition for the BIM Manager role and the specific responsibilities of different roles within different organisations may vary – hence a BIM Manager may or may not have operational responsibilities.

BIM Protocol   The CIC BIM protocol is used on BIM Level 2 projects, guiding clients to embed the contractual requirements for BIM within the project team's contract documents.

BIM Toolkit   The BIM Toolkit is a BIM project management tool that manages deliverables, coordinates responsibilities and fulfils the requirements of a Digital Plan of Works within a BIM Level 2 project.

Built environment sector   Describes those required to implement BIM Level 2. As of 2016, BIM Level 2 is mandatory for every centrally procured development project in the UK, so this sector includes utilities, construction and transport infrastructure.

CDE/Common Data Environment   The single source of information for a BIM Level 2 project. The CDE's function is to manage the storage and sharing of information between project team members during a project.

Clash detection   Also known as clash avoidance. Clash detection is the process of bringing together models from different disciplines in order to assess whether conflicts exist between the designs, so that they can be resolved prior to construction.

COBie/Construction Operations Building information exchange   A means of storing information that is to be shared across the project team and passed into the AIM upon completion of the project. COBie can be represented in XML format or as a spreadsheet.

Data drop   Also known as information exchange, usually a formal issuing of project deliverables at the end of a stage during a project. Specific data drop requirements are defined within a project-specific EIR.

DPoW/Digital Plan of Works   A project and information management tool used to define the project deliverables, the responsibility for completion, and the Level of Detail and Level of Information required at each stage.

Dynamic object   A digital object with parameters that may update in response to changes elsewhere in a model. This may cause the object to change shape or modify its specification in response to changes to other related aspects in the model, and is often referred to as an 'intelligent object'.

EIR/Employer's Information Requirements   The EIR defines specifically how BIM will be implemented on a project. It is used to define the requirements of the employer's technological and process management according to their Organisational Information Requirements, going through several iterations over the course of a project.

Enterprise resource planner   A software tool or suite of tools used for business management. Functionalities of different tools vary, but usually include resource planning, time monitoring, business intelligence, customer relationship management (CRM) and accounting.

External works   All the works that take place outside a building envelope, including infrastructure, utilities and landscape works.

Federated model   A model generated from the combination of several distinct models, often as exports from different software. Not usually editable and used for the purposes of design review and clash detection.

GSL/Government Soft Landings   A process used to ensure that built assets are in line with the needs of the users and managers of assets such as a landscape. It introduces an extended handover period and engagement with managers and users during the design phase.

IFC/Industry Foundation Classes   A non-proprietary data format developed for the purposes of information exchange on built environment projects.

IFD/International Framework for Dictionaries   A standard for the use of terminology on built environment projects. Can be used to define the scope of permitted uses for an information model and the processes used on a BIM project.

Landscape   All works that may be within the remit of a landscape-based design project, including built objects and some aspects of infrastructure.

Lean construction   Adopted from lean manufacturing processes, a system for built environment design projects that minimises waste and maximises value. Waste is the unnecessary use of time, materials and effort; value is whatever is required by the employer.

LoD/Level of Definition – also Level of Development   Level of Definition or Level of Development describes the Level of Detail of an entire model, including the graphical as well as the information content of the model.

LoD/Level of Detail   The degree of graphical detail in the objects contained within an information model.

   The general Level of Detail refers to the level of development of a model. This means that a model delivered at a given project stage should be suitable for that stage; a general Level of Detail would require that at concept stage the models provided can be relied upon for their conceptual contents, for example. Component Level of Detail refers to the specific level of graphical detail and information required for specific components.

LoI/Level of Information   The degree of non-graphical detail in the objects contained within an information model.

Lonely BIM   Also known as Level 1 BIM: implementing BIM processes and technology, but not sharing models or working to the BIM Level 2 process with a project team.

MIDP/Master Information Delivery Plan   The project plan that brings together the TIDPs to define the programme, responsibilities, protocols and procedures.

MPDT/Model Production and Delivery Table   Specifies the overall Level of Detail for models at each project stage.

Object   The virtual representation of elements and systems designed using software.

OIR/Organisational Information Requirements   An OIR informs specific AIRs and describes the information required by an organisation as a whole in order to operate its assets.

PDM/Project Delivery Manager   The PDM is the project manager with overall responsibility for the implementation of BIM on a project.

PDS/Product Data Sheet and PDT/Product Data Template   A standardised spreadsheet template for entering a manufacturer's or supplier's specification and sustainability information about a variety of construction products to facilitate information exchanges, particularly COBie. The completed PDT is referred to as Product Data Sheet (PDS).

PIM/Project Information Model   The information model that describes the asset during design and construction. May be produced as a series of drawings, models and files. Changes name to become the VCM once the information model is handed over for construction.

PIP/Project Implementation Plan A project or task team's statement defining their BIM, IT and human resources availability and capability for a specific project.

PLQs/Plain language questions A series of questions used as the basis of developing various information requirements and the GSL strategy. At each project stage these questions are revisited, answered and refined as necessary.

Responsibilities matrix The project-specific tool used by those responsible for project management to assign roles and responsibilities for the production of deliverables and the delivery of tasks to task teams.

Standard Methods and Procedures Standard Methods and Procedures define the core requirements of information management requirements for a project, including how the information management roles are defined on a project, naming strategy for files, spatial coordination strategy, and drawing sheet templates.

Task team A sub-team of the wider project team responsible for project delivery of a specific aspect of the project. The task team may be defined by discipline or consultant.

TIDP/Task Information Delivery Plan The project plan that defines an individual task team's responsibilities for the production of information.

VCM/Virtual Construction Model A term used to describe the PIM once it has been approved for the basis of construction works.

Volume A volume is a defined 3D space within a BIM project allocated to task teams.

Index